African Odyssey

African Odyssey

◆

The adventurous journeys of a Peace Corps volunteer in Africa

Floyd Sandford

To my friends at Terrace Glen.
All best wishes for good health
and happy times.

P. Sandford

July 14, 2022

iUniverse, Inc.
New York Lincoln Shanghai

African Odyssey
The adventurous journeys of a Peace Corps volunteer in Africa

iUniverse books may be ordered through booksellers or by contacting:

iUniverse
2021 Pine Lake Road, Suite 100
Lincoln, NE 68512
www.iuniverse.com
1-800-Authors (1-800-288-4677)

ISBN: 978-0-595-44017-7 (pbk)
ISBN: 978-0-595-88338-7 (ebk)

Printed in the United States of America

Contents

List of Illustrations

Preface

In 1964, at a time of uncertainty in my life, and with the Vietnam War raging, I joined the United States Peace Corps and went to West Africa, where I lived and worked as a science teacher for two years. The time I spent teaching and traveling in Africa represented two of the most memorable years of my life, filled with challenges and wonderful times.

Have you ever contemplated becoming a teacher? If you already are a teacher, have you ever imagined sharing your talents and abilities with deserving students in another country and culture? Have you thought about becoming a Peace Corps volunteer, of helping foster a global community based on greater mutual respect and understanding, instead of aggression and shallow political rhetoric?

Have you ever dreamed, as I did, of going to Africa, of opening a door leading to a different room in a wonderfully different place, of retracing steps and taking a road untaken?

If you can answer "yes" to any of these questions, or if you are simply curious about the story of a naive New Yorker who went to Africa and came to realize that the world is an exciting place, too large to be completely savored in a human lifetime, then perhaps you will enjoy this story of my African odyssey.

FS, Cedar Rapids, Iowa, January 2007

1

An African Odyssey Begins, May 1964

After a long flight, the Ethiopian Airlines jet landed, the hatch doors opened, and we disembarked into the steamy mammalian moistness of a West African evening. It was May 11, 1964, and I was setting my feet on the African continent for the first time, a childhood dream finally realized. We arrived at Lagos International Airport, Nigeria, at 10 pm. There had been recent heavy rains and in the short distance walking to the terminal, clothes quickly became sweat drenched and body clinging. Crossing the wet, puddled tarmac, like a large flock of dazed, disoriented sheep, we entered waiting vans. That's when the excitement began.

The Nigerian driver left the parking area in a manner reminiscent of the start of the Indianapolis 500. Within minutes, the van was barreling along streets teeming with throngs of pedestrians, taxis, and people on bicycles and motorbikes. It was approaching midnight, yet it seemed like nearly every inhabitant of Lagos was either lining, crossing, or traveling the same streets as our speeding van. There were no sidewalks, and crowded shops and market stalls were located close to the road's edge. People were walking roadside, sitting or standing in conversation, gathered around fires and cooking pots, or selling food and merchandise from stalls, pushcarts, trays secured by straps around their necks, or containers on their heads.

Women with huge woven baskets filled with cords of firewood, adroitly balanced on their heads, stood poised roadside, madly dashing across the street at the slightest breaks in traffic. Bicycles and motorbikes surrounded the van on all sides, darting every which way, coming within inches of our vehicle. Why were we traveling so fast? What were all these Nigerians doing out on the streets so late at night? Not once did we stop for a stop sign or a traffic light; there weren't any.

Plummeting through the kaleidoscopic maelstrom about me, I felt as if we'd suddenly been transported back in time to the hysteria of Bedlam, or dropped into one of Dante's circles of hell. When we finally arrived at the Niger Palace Hotel in Yaba, I couldn't believe we had reached our destination without leaving any fatalities or mangled bodies in our wake.

Jet lag, the excessive speed of our van, and the darkness of night prevented me a true picture of the reality of Lagos, Nigeria's capital in the 60's, and today one of the world's twenty largest cities. At dawn the following day I fully experienced the fevered blends of exotic odors; chaotic street scenes; incessantly-honking taxis; people, burdened and slowed by heavy loads carried atop their heads, dashing across busy streets; rough roads bordered by open sewers, and traders hawking their wares, dressed in brightly colored wrappers and dashikis.

While our group milled about in the hotel lobby, Nigerian desk clerks slowly checked us in, assigning rooms and issuing keys. Nigerians in vans transporting our luggage arrived and began unloading bags. After getting my room key and retrieving my two suitcases from the lobby luggage heap, I began my search for room 302. When I finally found it, I opened the door, turned on the lights, and dozens of cigar-sized cockroaches, festooning the walls, scurried into the nearest available crack or crevice.

At check-in, the desk clerks had instructed us to gather in a dining hall. Dropping my suitcases on the floor of my room, I went downstairs and found a seat in a large cavernous room with a single long table and eighty uncomfortable wooden chairs. I surveyed my surroundings as other members of the group filtered into the room and found seats. We presented a sorry sight, in our damp, wrinkled clothes, looking half asleep or glassy eyed.

We waited for nearly an hour, tired, disoriented, thirsty and famished, anticipating our first taste of authentic African cuisine. The table was bare except for several glass pitchers of water. There were no drinking glasses, napkins, dishware, or utensils, just the water pitchers. Was the water meant for drinking? Like everyone else, I was thirsty, having lost about a quart of body fluids through perspiration since leaving the plane. Could we drink the water? Was it safe? Had it been boiled? Nobody knew. Nobody was telling. Where were the in-country Peace Corps administrators who had briefly met us at the airport, but hadn't reappeared since we entered the waiting vans for our thrill ride through Yaba? There was a sense of unreality about my new surroundings. Had I really arrived in Africa, so far away from what I knew as home? Was I ready to spend two years in this new and different place?

Sounds of people yelling and pans banging emanated from a nearby kitchen, but there was no sign of a waiter, or word as to the reason for the delay. Finally, after midnight, two Nigerian men marched in carrying a large covered platter.

They sat the platter down in the middle of the table and ceremoniously lifted the metal dome-shaped lid, releasing a steamy cloud. The steam cleared. Voila!—there it was; a large pile of hot chicken heads! Wet, boiled, steaming, feathered, chicken heads. For most of the heads, the beaks and eyes were closed, but, in some, eyes and beaks were garishly open, as if decapitated and scalded in a moment of surprise and great anguish. Everyone sat staring at the mini-mountain of heads on the platter. The late hour, the strange surroundings after a day of exhausting travel, the steaming pile of chicken heads, was too surreal.

"Do those look like chicken heads to you?" someone from the far end of the table queried.

A volunteer, Carol, nearer the platter, moved in for closer inspection. "They sure look like chicken heads to me."

"Just chicken heads?" one person said. "That's it," another replied.

"Maybe there's something underneath, some legs or thighs maybe," someone yelled.

"Check underneath," and someone did. "Nope, solid chicken heads."

"Is this a joke?" someone said. "Could be some kind of elaborate table decoration," said another.

I tended to vote with the "fowl heads centerpiece" hypothesis, until the thought occurred to me that perhaps this was another perverse test; one last check by Peace Corps Washington to see if we could cut the mustard; one final test to see if we could adjust to the shock of new cultural circumstances without cracking up.

More time passed in idle banter, reflecting various degrees of disorientation, disbelief, or astonishment. No further food was forthcoming from the kitchen. Soon, the steam rising from the severed heads ceased. So, it was chicken heads for supper, after all! There were several hundred heads on the platter, about five for each of us, if divided fairly. I have never been a fussy eater, and had decided long before our plane landed in Africa that I would not spend the next two years in Nigeria as a transplanted ugly American, seeking out, even demanding, the replication of conditions and circumstances to which I was accustomed. I was prepared to try everything, to let Africa sweep over me as a wave in whose currents I would be agreeably transported. I was primed to go with the flow. But a pyramid of steaming chicken heads, late at night on an empty stomach, seemed too high a price to pay for cultural assimilation. I passed on the meal, and so did everyone else. It was a terrible waste of food, a reality check for both us and the cooks, but I assume someone or something ate the heads.

I was later informed that the proper etiquette for consuming cooked chicken heads is to pick up said head, pry open the beak, bring the opened beak to one's mouth and then, applying the necessary suction, suck out the brains. I'll take their word for it. All I know is that in two years of living in Africa, I never saw anyone eating chicken heads, properly or otherwise. Still, I have no doubt that someone, somewhere, eats chicken heads. It would be foolish to let chicken brains go to waste, especially in a West African country like Nigeria, where dietary protein deficiency is a major concern.

At first, every new situation and circumstance seems more daunting than it really is, and by the next morning most members of our group appeared ready to face the challenges of a new day. During our two-day orientation and lodging at the Niger Palace, we visited nightclubs and learned to dance the African highlife. We sampled uniquely different cuisine, like plantain fried in palm oil ("dodo"), which I immediately enjoyed, and ground cassava ("gari"), which I found tasteless. After a traumatic introduction to esoteric African dishes and unfamiliar surroundings on day one, I quickly regained my balance, and for the remainder of my stay in Africa, adjusting to unique social circumstances or trying new plant or animal foods was rarely a problem. Regardless of what the animal was, be it pygmy goat, monkey, snake, locust, or snail, I sampled them all, all except for goat head soup and cow foot stew. However, my cosmopolitan tastes extended only to animal muscular systems. Whenever I encountered other body parts, especially internal organs, such as hearts, intestines, testicles—and chicken brains—my response was to balk or gag.

Following my eye-opening first experience in African dining, a non-supper of steamed chicken heads, I climbed several flights of stairs at the Niger Palace at one am, tired and hungry. Room 302, sleeping quarters for my first night in Africa, consisted of a large sparsely furnished room with bare concrete walls illuminated by stark neon lighting. There were two beds equipped with mosquito netting, a clothes rack with no clothes hangers, and a single ceiling fan. I removed my damp clothes and collapsed on the bed, leaving my suitcases unopened on the floor where I had dropped them hours earlier.

That night I lay on sweat-soaked sheets on a too-short bed in a bleak room, anxious and apprehensive. Unable to sleep, yet physically exhausted, I was on an emotional roller coaster. My brain was wide awake, neurons firing. What had I done? Was I ready to live in Africa, so far from Long Island, for two whole years? Everything seemed so foreign to all that I had known. Tonight a platter of chicken heads; what might happen tomorrow? What had I gotten myself into?

As I tossed and turned, listening to the sounds of traffic noise, human laughter, music and incessant drumming outside my window, and the fluttering chitinous wings of strange flying insects colliding with the blades of the slowly-revolving ceiling fan, my thoughts turned to the events of the past year, and the circumstances that had led me to my strange and exotic new surroundings.

2

Southern Illinois, August 1963

It was typical August afternoon weather for Southern Illinois, oppressively hot and muggy. The air hung motionless and heavy, not a leaf moving, quiet save for the incessant droning of stridulating cicadas. I was at my desk in the laboratory of the Cooperative Wildlife Research Unit at Southern Illinois University in Carbondale. Quail censusing, a common late autumn chore for all the graduate students at the unit, was scheduled to start in several weeks. This would be my last quail census. I was not going to miss plodding across fields and pastures, marching up and down spoil banks and through bramble patches, in an unbroken line from dawn to dusk, for several days, counting all the quail in flushed coveys.

With quail census looming, I was continuing my work on foxes, as part of my research assistantship. The freezers at the unit were filled with dead red foxes (*Vulpes fulva*) and gray foxes (*Urocyon cinereoargenteus*). Most were road kills, their legs tagged with the date and place where they were struck by vehicles on southern Illinois highways. There seemed to be an endless supply of frozen foxes in the freezers, and when I wasn't skinning them for the unit's skin collection, I was identifying and categorizing stomach contents in a white enamel pan under a dissecting microscope. That day I was continuing my analysis of fox year-round feeding habits. I positioned the microscope, emptied the contents of yet another stomach into some water in a white enamel tray, and began sifting through hair clumps, mouse ears and feet, persimmon seeds, insect body parts, and other food items that gave evidence of what that fox had eaten on the day it met its inglorious end. A colleague, Don, sat across from me, and as we worked we talked about my roommate problems.

"You and Rich don't seem to be getting along too well lately," Don said.

"No," I replied, "and the latest situation has brought matters to a head."

I proceeded to tell him about the opossum incident that had occurred days earlier. Rich and I were alike in many ways, quiet, introverted, and intensely private types. We kept different study and sleeping schedules, and were seeing the same woman, the singer at the Flamingo lounge piano bar in downtown Carbondale, at the time. A number of factors had caused the relationship to sour, and it had been going steadily downhill for months, so that now we were cooking and eating alone, and rarely talking to one another in the small rental house we shared together. I had been thinking about leaving and finding a small apartment of my own for some time, but figured I could hold out for the few more months required to finish up all the obligations for my graduate degree. The opossum incident changed all that.

Several months earlier, Rich found a small opossum in the woods while he was squirrel hunting, and for some reason decided to become its surrogate parent. He brought it back with him and allowed it free run of the house. Rather than let it become yet one more source of tension and ill will I gritted my teeth and let him keep his pet, assuming that eventually the novelty would pass. Weeks went by, and I found the little monster eating my food in the kitchen, and leaving evidence of its wanderings all over the house.

"Rich, don't you think it's about time you let the opossum go? I don't think it's healthy to have a wild opossum living in the house, and I've grown weary of finding its turds on my bed."

"No, I intend to keep it for a while longer. If it's a problem for you, just close your bedroom door when you leave in the morning," he replied.

And so the mean-mannered marsupial remained a house guest for several more weeks, a constant irritant, and ever present reminder, of the animosity we felt towards one another. Rich allowed it free range of the house, except my locked bedroom, until that fateful morning. Rich left for work early, and as I walked bleary-eyed into the bathroom and was about to sit down on the toilet, I stopped in mid-crouch. There in the toilet bowl, wet, angry, and hissing up at me, was the possum, mad as hell at its predicament. I felt no sympathy for the little beast, and reached down and picked it up by its long naked tail, being careful not to let it bite me. Dripping wet, and hissing all the while, I carried it to the kitchen door and tossed it into the back yard.

"Free at last, back to nature you go," I called, as it scurried in the direction of some trees.

Later that evening a suspicious-looking Rich confronted me in the living room of the house as I was studying for an ichthyology exam.

"Have you seen possum?" he said.

"Not lately," I replied, offering as honest and non-prejudicial an answer as I could muster.

The following day, after my exam, as I was examining and cataloging the contents of another fox stomach, I was talking to Tom, a friend and fellow graduate student, in one of the back rooms at the research unit. I told him about my unexpected early morning possum-in-the-toilet bowl encounter, and as we were laughing about circumstances leading to the animal's liberation, who should suddenly appear in the doorway and engage me with a stare that could bend a nail, but Rich. He had been outside the door listening to my telling the story, and his face was beet red and contorted with anger. If looks could kill, I would have been a dead man.

He said nothing, but held his arms straight at his sides, fists clenched, then turned and walked away. I moved out of the house the next day. I found a small basement apartment, where I spent my last months in Carbondale. I shared the house with several others, including two students from South Vietnam, Mr. Sun and Mr. Truong, who introduced me to the small community of Vietnamese students studying at SIU at the time. Every morning we cooked and ate breakfast together, always the same meal of fried rice with eggs and onions.

The requirements for my MS degree in wildlife management were nearly completed. My thoughts were focused on the new year, and roads untaken. I had dreamed of going to Africa ever since a young boy. While working at the research unit, I decided that I did not want a career as a wildlife manager after all. I was confused and uncertain about my future direction, unwilling to commit myself to further graduate study, and unenthusiastic about the prospect of going to Viet Nam to kill total strangers. The decision to join the Peace Corps and go to Africa had taken shape and begun to grow during my last year at SIU.

Prior to my graduation from Smithtown High School I had traveled little beyond the confines of Long Island, with the exception of occasional visits to New York City. During my four years attending St. Lawrence University in upstate New York I saw little of the world beyond the borders of New York state, except for one late night trip to Montreal with some fraternity buddies hoping to hook up with loose women.

Following graduation, I spent a summer in Wyoming working with the Student Conservation Program. I assisted different researchers working on biology projects at the research station in Jackson Hole National Park. That summer experience exposed me to a wide array of new and wonderful outdoor adventures.

I accompanied world famous animal behaviorist Margaret Altmann on horseback trips into the back country of Jackson Hole, my first time on a horse. I learned about her studies of lesbian behavior in elk, and joined her for supper, backpacker potatoes cooked in a large iron pot over a campfire. She shared mesmerizing stories of her life and travels as we dined beneath a spectacular display of stars in the Wyoming night sky. I helped a researcher from the University of Kansas, by observing and recording the behavior of hoary marmots. I assisted another scientist who was studying digger wasps. I positioned myself by wasp burrows, watching for returning wasps carrying paralyzed prey. When the wasps landed, and before they had opportunity to enter their burrow openings and carry the prey to their underground chambers, I marked them on the thorax, for purposes of individual identification, with a small dab of paint.

One of my major responsibilities was assisting a University of Wyoming biology professor who was investigating the relationships between elk populations, gopher tunneling activities, and soil erosion at high altitudes. On horseback, leading two pack horses, we journeyed into the back country of Yellowstone National Park, not seeing other human beings or signs of civilization for weeks at a time. My wilderness experiences that summer, including a heart-pumping early morning up-close-and-personal physical encounter with a curious black bear, while sleeping alone on the banks of the Snake River, that left my sleeping bag perforated with dozens of claw marks, had whetted my appetite for far flung travel and new adventures elsewhere.

Like many other Americans I was inspired by John Kennedy and idealistic enough to believe in Peace Corps goals. And, selfishly, it was an opportunity for international travel, and the chance to visit a continent I had long dreamed about at a crossroads time in my life. By November of 1963 I had already turned down two Peace Corps assignments to West African countries because of scheduling conflicts. My thesis had been completed and accepted, and I was finishing up projects and planning to be home in New York by Christmas.

On November 21, I received a letter from Sargent Shriver, Director of the Peace Corps, informing me that I had been chosen as a promising applicant to enter a Peace Corps training project. I had five days to respond. Final selection for overseas service as a volunteer, the letter informed, would only be conferred if I was medically fit, of good character (as determined by a background investigation), successfully completed the training program, and was judged suitable for overseas assignment. Thus far, five out of six applicants accepting invitations to training had qualified for overseas service.

Details of my actual assignment arrived the following day. I was working on a report in my office when a Western Union telegram arrived. Sent November 22 at 1211 EST it read:

"I am happy to inform you that you have been chosen to participate in a Peace Corps training program for Nigeria in Education. Training begins in February. Details follow by letter. Congratulations". Sargent Shriver

That day, that moment, is one still vividly etched in my memory, for it was only minutes later that I sat in stunned disbelief listening to radio reports announcing the assassination of President John F. Kennedy in Dallas. I had great admiration for Kennedy, the president, scholar, and visionary. I knew nothing then of his weaknesses and personal faults as a fellow imperfect human being. I considered the Peace Corps to be a noble experiment, an example of the kind of leadership and assistance our country could be, should be, offering as hope to a world full of people less favored and fortunate. As I listened to news reports of the death of the man who had conceived the idea of the Peace Corps, I felt sick and empty.

Nigeria, in West Africa, was not my first choice for assignment location, but I decided not to delay my African adventure by turning down this third offer, awaiting an assignment to a wildlife-rich East African country that might never come. I said goodbye to Southern Illinois just before Christmas, and headed to Long Island to spend the holidays with my family. I was already living and working in Africa when I graduated from SIU *in absentia* with a MS degree in wildlife management in the summer of 1964.

I always wanted to be a biologist when I grew up

During my childhood, as early as I can remember, I was fascinated by animals, and sensitive to their plight at the hands of persecuting humans. There was a meadow and a woodland behind my home on Long Island, where I spent many hours exploring nature. Alone in the woods, I observed the antics of gray squirrels for hours. In the grassy meadow, there were wild daisies, buttercups, black eyed susans, wild strawberries, and an abundance of butterflies, grasshoppers, and field crickets. I knew of several different box turtles living there, and surveyed the kinds of butterflies and caterpillars on the milkweed and other meadow plants. I can recall spending much of an afternoon watching ants at an anthill.

Neither of my parents had any involvement with biology, animals, or nature generally, but they never said or did anything to discourage my interest and inclinations. Our house and small backyard, on the street of a typical Long Island neighborhood, assumed an animal farm atmosphere. Outside the house were rabbit hutches and an enclosure for a flock of hens; inside there were parakeets, tropical fish, domestic house mice, and hamsters. On our patio I built an enclosure containing large black ants. I collected red ants, added them to the arena, and charged smaller neighborhood children five cents to watch the ant fights.

At various times growing up, I cared for a wide assemblage of organisms: box turtles, newts, toads, wolf spiders, aquaria with developing frog eggs, fiddler crabs which I collected from the salt marshes at Stony Brook, metamorphosing caterpillars, hatching praying mantis egg cases, injured birds, moss and fern-filled terrariums creating a jungle habitat for anoles, and terrariums filled with carnivorous plants like Venus fly traps and sundews. One summer I spent several days diligently caring for a nest of baby rabbits that a neighbor discovered while mowing grass. I was unaware that they couldn't survive on cow's milk and was devastated when they died.

When I was twelve I vividly remember silently watching in awe, as a large harmless bull snake slowly slithered up the trunk of a big oak tree in my neighbor's back yard, only to run home cursing and screaming when the Philistine emerged from his garage with an axe and decapitated the beautiful creature. Whenever I visited the Smithtown public beach on the north shore of Long Island, I walked the shoreline rescuing beached or overturned horseshoe crabs, returning them to the water, at the same time that other people were battering them to death with rocks.

My first job, at thirteen, was working weekends as a farmhand at Nicodemus Farm, a small scale hobby farm in Nissequoque, not far from my home in Smithtown. It was owned by an absentee wealthy businessman living in New York City. My work included feeding buckets of oats to the two horses and cleaning the barn, hand milking the one cow then straining the milk through cheesecloth before refrigeration, tending to a small flock of sheep with one ornery ram, and taking care of the chickens.

I enjoyed reading adventure books involving travel and exploration, including those about "bring em back alive" Frank Buck. I secretly imagined myself as a modernized Frank Buck type when I grew up, bringing back alive exotic animals to delight zoo visitors. I always enjoyed visiting the Bronx Zoo with my father, one of the few activities I can recall us doing together, and imagined myself a famous zoologist and adventurer, traveling the globe and visiting strangely different and exotic places, discovering rare, even unknown, animals.

3

New York City

The Peace Corps training program for the volunteers in Nigeria X was held from February 6 to April 29, 1964 at Columbia Teacher's College in New York. Traveling from Smithtown to Penn Station in Manhattan on the Long Island Railroad, I checked in at the Paris hotel on 96th street, home for the next twelve weeks. There were nearly one hundred of us from all parts of the country

On the second day of the program, while still adjusting to our new circumstances and surroundings, we were required to take a battery of exams. Testing began early in the morning and continued into the late evening. There were five different psychological exams, including the MMPI (Minnesota Multiphasic Personality Inventory), the last test administered at the end of the ordeal. Most of us were both physically and mentally drained near day's end, and unenthusiastic about the prospect of a late supper, followed by yet more test taking into the late evening.

The MMPI consists of incomplete sentences, and calls for filling in blanks with the first thoughts that come to mind. Some volunteers like my new friend Ray didn't take the questions as seriously as they should have, responding with off-the-cuff comments reflecting a zonked out mental state and a reaction to testing overload. Ray responded with flippant answers to the questions, such as: When I look at my mother *I see a werewolf.* Or, When I am happy *I offer a toast to the mind of God.* That sort of thing. Little did he know at the time, but he was to pay for his playfulness later. The psychologists hired to evaluate our mental state and ascertain our fitness to adapt and successfully function in a new culture, and presumably also not embarrass the USA once abroad, took our test responses seriously—very seriously.

Early in the program, rumors spread that one among us was a CIA plant, looking to discover less than loyal Americans, perhaps even a communist sympathizer or two. Many of us had friends and family who had been interviewed by the FBI as part of our background checks, so the idea of a CIA mole amongst us had a certain ring of believability. During one of our full group meetings in a large auditorium at Columbia, one woman that none of us recognized, stood up in the back of the room and made incoherent rambling comments about American diversity and cultural insensitivity that left everyone puzzled. This woman never resurfaced again, and the grapevine had it that she had jumped into the East River. Rumors proliferated like hyper-sexed hamsters. No one knew what the staff persons were looking for in their quest to separate the fit from the unfit.

During the training program's first week, our large group was divided into smaller subgroups, each with its own assigned psychologist and psychiatrist. My psychiatrist, a Dr. Hornick, was a real character. He wore a plaid suit with a cape over his portly frame, and in keeping with the image of the great detective, a Sherlock Holmes hat and pipe look-alike. He entered a room with a flourish and a dramatic sweep of his cape, definitely weird. According to the rumor mill, he had been married and divorced four times. And this was the person destined to ascertain our mental stability and potential adjustability to the rigors of living and teaching in a foreign culture?

Many in the group were paranoid. Periodically, during the training program, potential volunteers were "weeded out", having been deemed unsuitable for service abroad. One minute we would be having lunch with a fellow trainee in the cafeteria at Columbia, or talking to them in the elevator at the Paris Hotel, and the next minute they would be gone, vanished without a trace. "Deselection" it was called. They, and all their belongings, rapidly whisked away, presumably on a plane back to Pocatello, Idaho, or wherever. For some reason these deselected trainees—about twelve persons in all—were adjudged unsuitable for one reason or another. We were never told why, and generally it was impossible to figure, as most of them seemed happy, sane, well adjusted people. I was concerned about the fate of my friend Ray, but he had one factor in his favor. He was a physics teacher, and Nigeria was in desperate need of science teachers, especially in physics.

Three of us became good friends during the program, Ray, Don, and myself. I experienced only cursory contact with Dr. Hornick. I was required to attend only one small group meeting, and no follow-up one-on-one sessions. This was the minimum. Ray was not so fortunate. His psychologist required him to return again and again, to go over his test responses. Before long, he was analyzing ink blots and starting to question his sanity

A major purpose of the training program was to help us prepare for our teaching duties at Nigerian secondary schools, or, for the two PhD's in our group, at a university. Part of the training involved working as practice teachers at a school in

NYC, preparing lessons plans, and then actually teaching classes. I was assigned to work at George Washington High School under the direction of biology teacher Mr. Roth. I traveled from the Hotel Paris to the school by subway for several weeks and, as Mr. Roth instructed, prepared lesson plans on subjects of my choosing. I diligently worked on a lesson about frog biology, complete with hand-made visual aids, handouts with definitions of important biological terms, and a colorful labeled poster of a frog. I then delivered my frog lecture to a group of largely disinterested students. Afterwards, Mr. Roth counseled me that it was a poor choice of topic, as most students at George Washington High had no interest in frogs, and most had never seen one.

There were also weekly meetings with a biology teacher for the six of us in the group preparing to teach biology. Each week we met in a Columbia classroom to take—and then grade—New York State regent's biology exams. This exercise might have been helpful had we been training to teach biology in New York State, but did little to help us prepare for teaching in tropical West Africa. Never once during our meetings did we talk about Nigeria or Africa in general, about tropical biology, or African ecology, flora and fauna.

When not thinking about teaching, our minds were kept busy with other components of the training program. We were lectured by officials from the US State Department about the tenets of communism, how to deal with communists, or to counter communist propaganda should the need ever arise. A doctor from a local hospital, a specialist in the effects and treatment of snakebite, lectured us about the venomous snakes of Nigeria, and what to do if bitten. We were informed that about half of the snakes in Nigeria are poisonous, then sat through a lengthy slide show with pictures of mambas, cobras, boomslangs, puff adders, Gaboon vipers, and other dangerous serpents. We were informed about the effects of untreated snakebites, illustrated with images of discolored human appendages, swollen and covered with ulcerations. The snake lecture and slide show occurred one evening after supper. The graphically disturbing color photos resulted in averted heads, gag reflexes, and nauseated persons exiting the auditorium, heading to toilets to be ill.

In the event that we found ourselves stranded on a road in rural Nigeria because of car breakdown, we had twenty hours of training in the workings of automobiles and small engine repair. Weeks later, at mock graduation ceremonies, we received diplomas from the Automotive Evening Trade School and the Board of Education of the city of New York, asserting that we were trained (and presumably competent) in vehicle maintenance.

Because there was a possibility that some teachers might be asked to work with sport's programs as part of their school duties, we had instruction in Nigerian games and dances. We spent several afternoons learning the rudiments of soccer by dividing into teams and playing in Riverside Park.

With all the lectures, testing, and meetings, the training program kept us busy. When I had any free time, I left Columbia and explored Manhattan. I made frequent visits to Greenwich Village and several to Coney Island. Three others volunteers and I rented bicycles and spent a day riding through Palisade Park in Westchester. One Sunday, Ray and I decided to attempt to walk the entire perimeter of Manhattan island in a day. We set out early in the morning from the Hotel Paris, walked north to the Bronx, then down the East side, staying as close to the East River as possible. We reached the Battery, the southernmost tip of Manhattan, at four pm. My feet were aching badly, and when we got to Chinatown I finally quit and took the subway back to the hotel; Ray finished on his own. Two days before the end of the program, five volunteers and I went to an Irish bar on West 96th Street to celebrate. When the other bar patrons learned that we were Peace Corps volunteers about to leave for Africa, they all chipped in and bought us several rounds of drinks.

On graduation day, after surviving psychological testing, peer-reviews, periodic meetings with psychologists and psychiatrists, competency exams in our teaching areas, practice teaching in inner city schools, and scrutiny from all quarters, most of the "survivors" felt ready to deal with any crisis that might arise in Africa. With certificates indicating satisfactory completion of a course in vehicle maintenance, and 695 credit hours, including 300 hours in technical studies, 100 hours of African studies, 100 hours of language study (Yoruba in my case), and 15 hours in the study of the philosophy, strategy, tactics, and menace of communist systems, I and seventy-nine other Nigeria X teachers were on our way.

I felt fully prepared to dialogue with communists and superbly defend the American way of life, and spent the next two years anticipating a communist confrontation that never happened. What did happen, instead, was exposure to a plethora of cultural differences for which any off-site training program cannot adequately prepare. I knew the rules of soccer, how to teach frog biology to Bronx teenagers, and how to defend the American way of life in a confrontation with a communist, but I knew little about West African ecology and natural history, and virtually nothing about how to successfully teach science from a University of Cambridge syllabus in a society where animistic and superstitious beliefs strongly prevailed.

I was ignorant about the religion of Islam, and had no insights into Muslim culture. About half of all Nigerians practice Islam. In Muslim society the left hand is used for personal bodily functions and considered unclean. As a left-hander, it would have been useful to know about Muslim strictures regarding the use of the left hand, but no one had bothered to tell me, and I am certain that during my first months in Nigeria I offended many people by inadvertently offering them food or drink with my left hand. The 695 hrs in the training program had prepared me for bites delivered by Gaboon vipers and the details of Nigerian games and dances, none of which proved useful, but ill prepared me for living in a country where superstition was commonplace and where I encountered Muslims daily.

On our final day, after opening the sealed envelopes handed us and learning that we had successfully completed the training program and were officially going to Africa, Ray and I celebrated by downing a shared bottle of gin followed by three beers each.

4

Hello Lagos, Hello Ibadan

In the 1960's, Lagos was the capital of the young independent country of Nigeria. When I arrived in May 1964, I was accompanied by seventy-nine other Peace Corps volunteers from all parts of the United States, including four married couples. Our ages ranged from nineteen to seventy-one years.

When our Nigeria X group left the United States for Nigeria, nine other Peace Corps contingents had preceded us and over twenty more groups were to follow. In the 60's Nigeria had more Peace Corps volunteers (approximately 1900) than any other country, with the exception of India. There was a sense then that Nigeria was a shining hope for democracy in black Africa, and that an influx of Peace Corps teachers would assist the young country in its development goals.

An unfortunate incident involving a Peace Corps volunteer from Nigeria I, the first group to Nigeria, preceded our arrival. In October of 1961, a volunteer named Marjorie Michelmore wrote a postcard describing her location in Nigeria as one of "squalor" where living conditions were "primitive" and people went to "the bathroom in the streets." Intending to send it to a boyfriend in the States, she instead erringly dropped it on the University of Ibadan campus. It was found by a Nigerian student who made copies and distributed them campus-wide. The ripple effects from the ugly incident created tensions, but the publicity served a positive purpose of focusing American public attention on the economic and social problems facing the newly independent country and young democracy of Nigeria.

Our chartered TWA flight from Kennedy International Airport was my first time on a plane. During the trans-Atlantic crossing we were served a delicious dinner of wine and chateaubriand, and entertained by a James Bond movie, all courtesy of the Peace Corps. As a transition between the world I had known and the one I would experience for the next two years the luxury of the trip was memorable and inappropriate. Our plane stopped in Madrid where we transferred to Ethiopia Airlines and headed for Africa. We stopped briefly in Conakry, Guinea, and briefly debarked the plane. Peering through waves of heat rising from the runway, and beneath a painfully bright sun, I hastily took my first African photos, some over-exposed pictures of what appeared to be jungle far off in the distance across the tarmac. It was not until we landed in Lagos that I got my first real taste of Africa and the country that would be home for the next two years.

Following our evening arrival in Lagos, a midnight non-meal of chicken heads, and two days in Lagos sequestered at the Niger Palace, the Nigeria X contingent split into four sub-groups, each headed to the capitals of the four regions constituting the nation of Nigeria at that time (Ibadan in the Western Region, Benin in the Midwest Region, Enugu in the Eastern Region, and Kaduna in the Northern Region).

On May 13, 1964 my subgroup of eighteen volunteers traveled to Ibadan in the Western Region. Driving north from Lagos over one hundred miles of eroding road beds, passing through the city of Ijebu-Ode, we arrived in Ibadan and checked into rooms at the Rem Hotel, home for the next week. Most of us had received our provisional placements during the training program at Columbia. Expecting an assignment in the Western Region I had received instruction in Yoruba, the language of the Yoruba tribe, the dominant group in the region. Some volunteers, however, were victims of poor planning. Two volunteers preparing to teach English in the Northern Region had spent three months learning Hausa, only to be re-assigned at the last minute to teach math at schools in the Eastern Region, where the major language was Ibo.

Other examples of inefficient matching of volunteer with teaching assignment, or last minute changes in posting, were not uncommon. On a survey form, I had asked to be assigned to a school in a rural location, remote from civilization. As a biologist and nature lover, I wanted to experience natural ecosystems and be near wildlife. Instead, I was assigned to a school adjacent to a noisy and congested highway in the metropolis of Ibadan, at that time and still today, the largest city in Black Africa. In 1964, it had a population of about 640,000 people; now (in 2007) its population exceeds three million.

Whereas I wanted to "go bush" and went urban instead, two of the senior volunteers in our group, retired female English teachers in their late sixties, requested postings to a school in a location that offered some amenities such as comfortable housing with indoor plumbing, reliable transportation, and nearness to a good hospital. Contrary to their requests, they were sent to schools in remote villages—places like Ijebu-Igbo and Okitipupa—where they lived in Spartan accommodations with mud walls and dirt floors, and without electricity. Located many miles from their schools, they were issued bicycles for their commutes to work or trips to market. At the time it made no sense, but perhaps in the grand scheme of things the Peace Corps and the Nigerian Ministry of Education knew what they were doing. Ours was not to question why.

On May 14th our subgroup of eighteen traveled to Government House, located on a beautiful hilltop estate overlooking Ibadan. We were served coffee and biscuits and had an opportunity to meet, and have our pictures taken with, Chief 0. Fadunsi, Governor of the Western Region. The next day was filled with sightseeing tours of populous, sprawling Ibadan, a tour of the University of Ibadan, and a visit to the Ministry of Education. At the Ministry we met more Nigerian officials and had another photo session. Later in the week, after final confirmation of our teaching assignments, we said our goodbyes and left for our individual school sites. Another volunteer and I went to schools in Ibadan; the rest went to cities and villages elsewhere in the Western Region—Abeokuta, Badagry, Ilorin, Iseyin, Oyo, Oshogbo, and Ogbomosho.

We all reconvened at Government House in Ibadan the next month for a meeting with Chief Samuel L. Akintola, the unpopular Premier of the Western Region. More group photos. As I stood a step above and behind Premier Akintola for our group photograph I remember being impressed by his pronouncedly visible facial scars, three noticeably long and wide vertical marks on each cheek. Our group meeting with Akintola in Ibadan was the last time I saw most of the other PCV's in my group. For the next twenty-three months most of my social interactions were with Nigerians.

For someone who had requested assignment in the relative isolation and tranquility of the bush, my school posting came as a shock. I was assigned to teach science at Ibadan Boys High School (IBHS), located on noisy Ijebu Bye-Pass in the densely crowded Oke-Ado section of highly urbanized Ibadan. For most of my time in Nigeria I was destined to move amongst throngs of people and listen to the sounds of honking taxis, experiencing animal life no wilder than the domesticated pygmy goats that grazed on the school compound, or the agama lizards that scurried about the sidewalks or perched on walls and walkways, displaying to one another by push-ups and head-bobbing.

I settled into the lodgings provided for me by the school. My house was unexpectedly comfortable, and nicer than any of the three places I had stayed in as a graduate student in Carbondale. I had the entire top floor of a two-story home—Adeyoola Chambers—on Liberty Stadium Rd in the Oke-Badan section of Ibadan, about two miles from IBHS. A married Peace Corps couple, Ed and Helen Butt, who had arrived months earlier in Nigeria VIII, lived below me. My quarters consisted of a living room, three bedrooms, a bathroom with shower, a small kitchen, and a balcony overlooking the road. Except for two of the bedrooms, the house was nicely furnished. My bedroom had a standard-sized bed with mosquito netting, a large clothes closet, a small bedside table and lamp, and a small wooden cupboard with a lock and two keys.

I had electricity, running water, ceiling fans, a refrigerator, an electric stove, and a flush toilet. Water for drinking came from the kitchen tap, but was first boiled, then filtered. The house had large windows on the front and sides, all equipped with screens and slatted glass blinds. The windows could be opened to catch a breeze or closed during heavy downpours in the rainy season, or when dust-laded harmattan winds blew down from the arid north in the dry season.

Next to the house was an open shed with a metal roof where Ed and I kept our Honda 50 motorcycles. Fruit-bearing banana and papaya trees, colorful hibiscus, and bougainvillea plants, grew in the back and side yard. Access to the house was through a back door, reached by a set of concrete steps at the end of a walkway leading from the road that passed between the house and the motorcycle shed. When I was at home, the back door and the balcony door at the opposite end of the house were always left open for air circulation.

The front of the house was located only a few feet from Stadium Road, separated from it by an open sewer so typically found roadside in developing tropical countries. There were no sidewalks, pedestrians and people selling goods walked alongside the road. From my balcony and beyond the road, there was a patch of palm trees and low-growing vegetation obscuring a communal neighborhood water pump. A steady stream of neighborhood children visited the pump, emerging from the trees carrying basins and pails of water on their heads. A small stream littered with debris, carrying unhealthy-looking water, was nearby. When people cleaned their clothes on laundry days, the stream ran white with soap and detergents. Beyond this small area of stream, shrubs, and trees, there was a vast expanse of densely spaced houses with metal roofs as far as the eye could see, reflecting the crowded urban lifestyle of the Yoruba in Ibadan.

Below my balcony on Stadium Road there was an endless procession of taxis carrying people to Liberty Stadium for soccer games on game days, and to neighborhood bars and highlife clubs at night. From pre-dawn to late at night, a steady stream of pedestrians walked along both sides of the road. These included school children dressed in their official school uniforms, market women with infants strapped on their backs, carrying huge loads of firewood or yams in baskets expertly balanced on their heads, and adults and children hawking their wares from boxes, glass cases, or metal trays.

Within weeks of moving into Adeyoola Chambers I hired a cook-steward and acquired favored vendors who periodically appeared on my back porch. These included Bose the egg girl, who sold me guinea fowl eggs at three pence each, and Babatunde, my palm wine tapper, a young man who delivered palm wine every Sunday. There was intense competition for my business. Many other women periodically came to the house trying to sell me eggs. They were always good-natured and understanding when I told them that I had decided to buy all of my eggs from Bose.

One young boy about eight year old continually appeared at my back door trying to sell me his chewing sticks. He never made a sale, though I occasionally tipped him for his industry and perseverance. In the morning it was a common sight to see Nigerians walking to work or doing their chores with a chewing stick in their mouth. As it remained in the mouth, continuously manipulated and moistened, the wood fibers at the end of the stick separated, crudely resembling a brush. The frayed end of the stick was rubbed against the teeth in the manner of a toothbrush. I never learned the name of the kind of tree that supplied the wood used to make chewing sticks, but conjectured that the tree probably contained potent anti-bacterial chemical compounds, as most of my students had beautiful, cavity-free teeth. I meant to inform research scientists working at Colgate Palmolive or Bristol-Myers of my hypothesis upon returning to the States, but never did.

Other vendors periodically visiting the house included a girl who stopped weekly with her puff puff pastries, Mary, the girl selling fresh oranges, and the fried plantain woman who set up shop in the late afternoon by the motorcycle shed and was always there awaiting me when I returned from school.

The country of Nigeria

Nigeria (once called the Slave Coast) is a large country, over 350,000 sq. miles in area, on the coast of West Africa. It lies east of Ghana (once the Gold Coast) and further east still from the Ivory Coast, which still bears that name. Many Africans exported from Africa during the days of the slave trade came from Nigeria, or were carried away from sea ports located there. Nigeria is named from the Niger River, which begins more than one thousand miles to the east near Sierra Leone, passes through Timbuktu in Mali in the Sahara desert, then runs south through Nigeria, entering into the Atlantic at the oil-rich Niger delta at the Bight of Benin in the Gulf of Guinea. It was then, and still is, a British commonwealth country, granted independence on October 1, 1960. All education beginning at the secondary level is in English.

Climate and vegetation varies from a wet, lush eighty-mile wide belt of tropical rain forest along the coast, to savanna, to short grassland, and finally to desert conditions in the sub-Saharan North. Nigeria is a country of great diversity, with more than 250 ethnic and linguistic groups. Distrust and animosity based on tribal differences was a problem in the 60's and continues today. Many tribal groups are small, but three major groups comprise about half of Nigeria's current population (as of 2007) of over ninety million people: the Ibo (Igbo), living predominantly in the southeast, the Yoruba in the southwest, and the Hausa-Fulani in the north.

In the 60's, when I arrived, the countries three major cash crops were cocoa, groundnuts (peanuts), and palm oil. Minerals like tin and columbite were mined in the north.

In 1956 an event occurred that had a profound effect on Nigeria's future. In that year a crude "sweet" low-sulfur oil first gushed forth from the marshy ground of the Niger Delta, a discovery that was to change everything. In the 70's the Nigerian government nationalized the oil industry, Nigeria joined OPEC, and the federal budget began to bloat with petrodollars. The ensuing cancer of oil corruption brought immense wealth to a fortunate few. Roads and pipelines were built in the Niger delta, broken or leaking pipes contaminated waterways, fish populations suffered, and thousands of acres of mangroves disappeared.

Now (in 2007) Nigeria ranks as the world's sixth largest oil exporter, and 70% of the countries economy is based on annual oil revenues. The transformation from an agrarian to an oil-based economy ushered in a glut of greed, political and social instability, and mind-boggling environmental devastation. Oil has brought immense wealth to multinational oil companies and corrupt governmental officials, but social unrest and polluted and scarred landscapes to local communities.

Anyone who is delusional enough to still believe in the fantasy of trickle-down economics need only look at what has happened in Nigeria where a select few live lifestyles of obscene indulgence, and the majority of Nigerians are in worse shape today than they were in the 60's, when the flame of future promise for the country burned much more brightly.

Today, Nigeria no longer consists of four major regions as it did when I arrived in the 60's. The country is now divided into thirty-six states and the territory that includes the federal capital at Abuja. The legal system is based on English common law, except for the twelve northern states where Islamic law prevails.

Facial scarification among the Yoruba

In years past, facial scarification was a common practice among the Yoruba. Reasons for facial marks included: a traditional aspect of the culture; identification for persons of royal lineage; claims of ownership; as decoration to enhance beauty; identification of ethnic origin, or as a component of ritual to ward off evil spirits. Many different facial mark patterns were used by the Yoruba. Facial marks for beautification purposes were typically simple, perhaps only a few short vertical scars on the cheeks; those for identification purposes were usually more elaborate and extensive, and might involve numerous long scars, both horizontal and vertical, covering much of the face.

Many of the Nigerians I lived among or met in the 60's bore tribal facial scars, but the practice was fast disappearing then and is rarely, if ever, practiced now. A certain scar pattern existed for each specific province or locality in Yorubaland; thus, a person's village could be determined, and in earlier times lost children re-united with relatives. Tribal scars have less usefulness in the twentieth century.

Many boys at IBHS with facial marks were either embarrassed or unhappy because of them. Scarred boys were sometimes teased or ridiculed by their classmates. One of the most frequent questions I was asked by students in my biology classes was whether I knew of a way to erase facial scars.

5

Ibadan Boys High School

June 2, 1964 was a memorable day for two reasons. It was my first day of school, and also the day for the public release of a statement by the Revolutionary Council of the Nigerian Youth Congress threatening to wage war against the US Peace Corps unless the Nigerian government began "a systematic and urgent withdrawal" of volunteers from the country. In part, the animosity that some Nigerians expressed towards the Peace Corps then was a vestige of the anger generated by the earlier Michelmore postcard incident in 1962. In a thirty-seven page booklet the Youth Council denounced Peace Corps volunteers as willing agents of neo-colonialism, military trained, and versed in espionage. As I sat nervously in the back of the assembly hall with the other masters, I contemplated the absurdity of anyone thinking me a CIA stooge or government agent.

At 8:20 am the opening assembly began. The principal entered the assembly hall wearing a black robe and mortarboard, and carrying books, accompanied by singing and ceremony. Everyone stood, the boys waving their hands above their heads, as S. Akintunde Lasiende, BA (Hons.) Lond. strode rather pompously to a dais on the bare stage. Then came the singing of the school anthem, written by the principal, who served in that capacity at IBHS from 1955-1972. The last line of the anthem was "Domini Opera Pro bono publico" (the works of God are for the good of the people), which was also the school's official motto.

After more hymns and a prayer, the principal summoned me to the front of the hall for introductions. As I stood awkwardly before the boys, he delivered a painfully long sermon on the virtues of studying hard and striving to succeed in life, using me as a prop. When he referred to me as "a young man of twenty-four with a Master's degree," some in the audience laughed. It was only later that I realized that many of the 5th form students in the secondary school of 310 boys were as old as I, or older. At twenty-four years of age, with a graduate degree, I would be teaching secondary school students, some of whom were older than myself.

I soon settled into a routine as a science teacher at IBHS. After one week both the Western Nigeria Director and Associate Director of the PC approved my request for a Honda 50 motorcycle, enabling me to more easily make the four mile round trip to and from work. My downstairs neighbor Ed taught mathematics at IBHS. We often drove to school together on our Honda 50's, always donning our regulation polo helmet for the ride through heavy traffic.

I usually arrived at school early, before 8 am. Tutors gathered in the staff room, next to the principal's office, before school started. There were ten of us, each assigned a personal desk All of the other teachers were Nigerians, like English tutors Mr. Onibonoje and Mrs. Odebunmi.

Most Peace Corps teachers in Nigeria were assigned posts at either missionary schools or government schools. My assignment at IBHS was somewhat unique, as it was a private school, the first private-owned school in Nigeria, founded in 1938. The school had a jaded reputation. The principal and the school manager were corrupt and in collusion, and many in the general public considered the boys attending the school to be low achieving thugs and troublemakers. During my entire two years working at IBHS, I never did meet the school manager, though he owned Adeyoola Chambers where I lived.

There were almost daily frustrations associated with teaching, prompting a frequently heard PCV lamentation of "WAWA" (West Africa Wins Again), but I plunged ahead, trying not to let frequent disappointments, school mismanagement and inefficiency, inadequate equipment, or the heat and humidity get me down. Within several weeks the principal appointed me head of the science department. This required me to be in charge of all the laboratory equipment and to be responsible for ordering any needed supplies and materials. Since the school had no chemistry teacher, it also meant that I was responsible for teaching all the chemistry classes, in addition to all the biology classes, at the school.

The rainy season, lasting roughly from April to October, had begun. Up to one hundred and fifty inches of precipitation could be expected, mainly in the late afternoon and evening. Heavy rains and high humidity created difficult working and living conditions. Many oppressive hot and humid nights I lay naked without covers in my bed, bathed in sweat, separated from the ever-present mosquitoes by netting. Loud repetitive drumming and highlife music coming from nearby nightclubs, and unfamiliar sounds emanating from the street and surrounding neighborhood, often made sleeping difficult.

I arrived in Africa with three pairs of long pants, six long sleeved dress shirts, several ties, and three pairs of expensive black leather shoes, anticipating dressing for a "professional look" while teaching. I quickly learned that such attire was totally inappropriate for the tropics, and took to wearing white shorts made by a tailor in the local market, a short sleeved casual shirt, and sandals made locally from reused car tires.

On one infrequent dress-up occasion, as I was preparing to attend an official Peace Corps function several months after arriving, I went to the closet where I had stashed the leather shoes. Opening the closet door, I discovered six amorphous mold and fungi covered lumps, a footwear gestalt. The fungal hyphae had overgrown the shoes and were extending outward onto the closet bottom. When I lifted the shoes I could see their shapes outlined on the floor. The biodiversity of fungi species, in a kaleidoscope of different colors, over-growing the leather in clumps and mats in the humid conditions of the closet was amazing to behold. Thus ended the brief life of my expensive leather shoes, two pairs never worn.

Gradually adjusting to new surroundings and the oppressively high humidity, I took my anti-malarial medicines faithfully and cultivated good relations with my neighbors.

Once I began teaching, I quickly realized that many boys in my classes were sick and in need of medical attention. The typical punishment meted out by the principal for students who had committed some infraction, was to remove them from classes and sentence them to grass cutting on the school compound. The students did this barefoot using machetes, often resulting in nasty cuts. Boys disobeying school rules were caned in the principal's office in the early morning before the start of school, then came to class with welts and bruises. Some boys had untreated skin sores or experienced malaria episodes during class.

When I realized that there was no one at the school to oversee the student's health care needs, and that the school didn't even own a first aid kit, I approached the principal and told him my concerns. He replied that first aid supplies were not a priority and that students at IBHS were responsible for their own health care. When I heard this I requested permission to set up a first aid cabinet at the school, and he told me that I could do so if I wanted. Not seeing it so much as my want but as an obvious school need, I went to a nearby pharmacy and purchased bandages, rubbing alcohol, calamine lotion, and other medical supplies, and set up a modest dispensary in a small storage room adjacent to the biology classroom. At the next school assembly I announced to all the students and teachers that a first aid station now existed at IBHS. Boys feeling ill or needing help could come to the room before morning classes began.

The next day I exited noisy and congested Ijebu Bye-Pass on my Honda and entered the drive leading to the school compound. When I reached the classroom block where I normally parked, I was greeted by a long queue of boys waiting outside the classroom door. Some had arrived an hour earlier in order to be first in line.

From that day forward I became the official school dispensarian, administering health care and purchasing medical supplies with funds from my monthly Peace Corps subsistence allowance. I made extensive use of gauze and bandages, calamine lotion, rubbing alcohol, and antibiotic ointments, and encouraged seriously ill boys to contact a family member and get proper medical care. Although I could recognize the symptoms of certain tropical diseases like schistosomiasis or malaria, I was not equipped or competent to treat these and other more serious health problems like high fevers or bleeding sores, but the boys were pleased just to have someone available who seemed interested in their ailments and willing to help.

One day in biology class, while lecturing about the anatomy and physiology of excretory systems, I mentioned some specific problems affecting the human urinary system. I told the students that a common worm parasite prevalent in Nigeria, and tropical Africa generally, was the blood fluke *Schistosoma haematobium*, the cause for the condition of urinary schistosomiasis, also called bilharziasis, or swamp fever.

After talking to the students about the symptoms of the disease and the effects of the parasite on the urinary bladder, a boy sheepishly approached me after class and told me that he had noticed blood in his urine. A relative had told him that it was because he was becoming a man (there is much ignorance and misinformation about schistosomiasis), but he now wondered if it could be because of the disease. I told him that there are several possible causes for blood in urine but that it would be interesting, and in the spirit of scientific inquiry, to investigate.

I asked the boy for a urine sample. I let the urine sit for an hour, allowing any worm eggs present to settle to the bottom of the bottle. Then I pipetted a sample from the bottom and put it on a glass slide. Examining the urine sample on the slide under a microscope, I found several schistosome eggs. Before school ended for the day I located the boy and showed him the results, encouraging him to tell his parents and have them consult a doctor.

When I learned that one of my students was infected with a serious parasite, I became curious about the overall incidence of the disease among all the students in my 5th form classes. The following day I informed all sixty 5th form students at IBHS about schistosomiasis. I told them about the worm's life cycle and how persons can become infected. I informed them of the symptoms of an infection, such as an itching sensation ("swimmers itch") after being in the water, a reaction caused by the infective larvae penetrating the skin, or blood in the urine caused by the presence of adult worms in the blood vessels around the bladder.

I asked all sixty boys to come to the biology laboratory after school and to give me a urine sample. I was greatly surprised when all of the students complied with my request. Upon examining their samples, I discovered that six of the sixty boys tested (10%) had schistosome eggs in their urine. Although I was working with an inferior microscope, and my methods were crude compared to the more precise techniques used in hospitals or diagnostic laboratories, I was not surprised to find such a high rate of infection. When I questioned them at the time they handed me their samples, many boys told me that in the past they had either gone swimming in rivers, or entered streams to bathe or fetch water.

During my two years running the dispensary I went through dozens of bottles of calamine lotion. I liberally applied the lotion for rashes, bruises, fever, and all sorts of real and imagined aches and pains. A frequently encountered affliction at IBHS was "brain fatigue," an ailment voiced by boys who felt overworked from the demands of excessive homework and study. For all brain fatigue sufferers I applied calamine lotion to their foreheads. Such calamine dabs soon became hallmarks that carried a certain amount of status ("Hey, everybody, look at me. I've really been working my brain").

The most difficult and frustrating cases to treat were boys with cuts and welts on their backs, buttocks, or thighs, from the almost daily canings that took place each morning in the principal's office. Caning was administered as punishment for a wide range of infractions, including vandalism and misbehavior, disobedience, not wearing the official school uniform or official school badge, or failure to pay school fees on time.

I never accepted the brutality of caning, and it was an underlying source of constant tension between the principal and me. Nearly every morning as I sat in the staff room adjacent to the principal's office I heard him reading off a list of complaints against some boy, followed by a pause when I envisioned his secretary urging the boy to bend over to receive the cane. The sound of a boy screaming as his buttocks and thighs were whacked often caused me to leave the staff room in disgust. It was such a depressing way to begin the teaching day. Many mornings I avoided the staff room altogether, working instead in the biology classroom on the opposite side of the compound. Boys caned for failure to pay school fees on time were ordered to leave school until they returned with the money. Those punished for other offenses spent all day with machetes cutting grass.

Ed and I were well accepted by the Nigerian teachers, and relationships were always congenial, though I had some friendly disagreements with portly Mr.

Osunyejo. The information and advice he gave the younger boys in his 2nd form nature study class often conflicted with facts I was giving students in my 3rd form general science class and my 4th and 5th form biology classes. According to Mr. Osunyejo "all lizards are poisonous," a statement I knew to be false, and "palm-wine was good for one's virility," a fact which might have been true, but hardly seemed good advice to be giving young boys who had enough problems to cope with besides that of alcohol abuse. One day, in the dispensary, a 2nd form boy came to me in tears, his entire body smeared in palm oil and turpentine, Mr. Osunyejo's treatment for skin rash.

Three months after my arrival, on Sept 10, 1964, the students participated in an all-school riot that made headlines in the local newspaper. Someone had damaged an electric meter at the school. When no one fessed up as the guilty party the principal levied a six pence fine on each of the 310 boys at the school. The next morning the boarding students boycotted breakfast and classes. Armed with sticks and stones, they looted the residence of one of the boarding house masters and punctured the tires on the principal's shiny big black Cadillac. From the relative safety of the staff room I watched the students in their generally peaceful protest, carrying placards accusing the principal and school authorities of financial malpractices, maltreatment and maladministration. Eventually the police were called, and the students dispersed. The next day the principal suspended all 185 boarding students and permanently dismissed ten students he identified as ring-leaders and general troublemakers. Three of the expelled students were 5th form boys preparing to sit for their West African School Certificate examinations in two months time.

School resumed after the riot, and my teaching duties kept me busy. Classes were occasionally disrupted by traffic accidents on nearby heavily trafficked Ijebu Bye-Pass, including horrific pedestrian-auto collisions. Market women slowed by heavy loads on their heads, attempting to cross the road, were sometimes hit by speeding taxis. On Ijebu Bye-Pass, as elsewhere in Nigeria, crossing a busy street was always risky business as vehicles had the right-of-way. On other occasions, classes were interrupted by political demonstrations, dramatic lightning storms, or by chickens or goats wandering into the classroom.

As time passed, I became increasingly familiar with native tropical flora and fauna. I joined a local naturalist group, consisting of other biology teachers in Ibadan, and went on several field trips into the countryside outside the city. I visited cocoa plantations, saw unusual fungi, chameleons, cashew trees, a wide variety of fragrant flowering plants, and trees adorned with the distinctive dangling nests of weaver bird colonies.

Because of limited funding for the science program, I often spent time before and after classes in the biology and chemistry classrooms fixing old or broken equipment. Often there wasn't enough time, so I sometimes came to school and worked on weekends. I cleaned off and repaired neglected wall charts that I found dust-covered and ripped in a disordered storage room. The school owned only several functioning microscopes; they were either filthy or faulty, so I did the best I could to make them workable. I made terrariums from pieces of scrap glass. Attempting to teach chemistry at IBHS was especially problematic, as important chemicals were missing from the supply cabinet, and needed laboratory equipment was unavailable or in short supply. Whenever I complained to the principal he always gave his stock reply of "no money."

How could there be no money? Boys were paying hefty school fees for academic and athletic equipment, yet the science laboratories lacked basic supplies, and the players on the school's official soccer team played barefooted because there were no funds for shoes. The biology laboratory lacked important learning aids like preserved specimens, aquariums, or anatomical models, and the chemistry laboratory had too few test tubes, and chipped or broken glassware. Any live plants or animals I wanted to use to illustrate a lecture had to be found and collected during my free time.

In December of 1964 I was required to administer the University of Cambridge West African School Certificate (WASC) exam in biology for the 5th form boys, most of whom had been taught their biology from the former science teacher at the school. An important component of the exam is a practical, requiring biological specimens that the students are asked to identify, sketch and label, or otherwise study during the exam. All preparations for the exam are conducted in absolute secrecy, of course, and a week or so before the exam the principal handed me the sealed envelope containing the list of necessary materials that I had to have ready for that year's practical exam. In a larger and better equipped government school or a well-funded and well-organized mission school, such preparation might not have been a problem, but at IBHS it meant panic and near crisis. Without any help or school support I had to solve any problem by myself, and to prepare for the upcoming WASC exam I spent the next week frantically trying to find and accumulate fifty hibiscus stems, fifty mammal tibias, and fifty cockroaches. Securing the stems and the roaches proved relatively easy, but rounding up fifty mammal shin bones required creativity and several trips to bone heaps in the native market where goats were slaughtered

Rarely did the teaching ever go smoothly. There was always some crisis to contend with, some problem to solve. If a Nigerian teacher failed to come to school there were no substitute teachers available, and boys sat idly at their desks or created mischief. It bothered me to see students, whose extended families had pooled together the necessary funds to pay the fees for a boy's education, sitting in a teacher-less classroom, so during my free periods I often entered such unattended rooms, asked what the subject was, and commenced teaching. I was totally unqualified and unprepared to teach that day's lessons in civics, Latin, or Nigerian history and government, but gave it a go anyway because it pained me to see boys short-changed on their education.

In addition to class work there always seemed to be something at the school that needed doing, whether it was treating an injured student, assisting in organizing the school literary magazine, helping out the school's soccer team, or tackling my responsibilities as a boarding house master. Problems, like the brooms of the sorcerer's apprentice, seemed to multiply. But somehow, in some way, each problem that arose was overcome. Days sleepily passed, one into another, and the unhurried casual pace of living in the tropics made me almost oblivious to the passage of time.

Schistosomiasis

Schistosomiasis is one of the major parasitic diseases affecting humankind, and along with malaria, tuberculosis and AIDS, is a major public health concern in Africa. One public health fact emphasized during the Peace Corps training program was that volunteers should never enter any fresh water lakes, rivers, or streams while in Nigeria, or Africa generally, as nearly all freshwater bodies on the continent contain infected snails that carry schistosomiasis. Development schemes such as irrigation projects, dams, or rice and fish farming, can contribute to an increased number of unsafe water sources.

The trematode flatworm responsible for the condition has a complicated life cycle. Humans are infected when they enter fresh water sources that have snails carrying the infective intermediate stage. The immature stage, or cercaria, leaves the snail, swims through the water, and enters the skin of humans who are bathing, washing, or swimming. Once in the body, larval forms grow and develop into adult worms that live in blood vessels around the urinary bladder. Mature fertilized eggs produced by female worms leave the body in urine. If the urine finds its way into a freshwater lake or stream the eggs hatch, the larvae infect a snail host, and the life cycle is completed. A person with urinary schistosomiasis releases worm eggs when they urinate, and if the infection is great enough, there can also be blood in the urine.

6

Hot Stuff!—My First Dinner Invitation

During my two years in Africa several members of Nigeria X left the country early, for health or personal reasons, or for causes unknown to me. While conditions at IBHS often seemed intolerable, and there were many discouraging days when I was convinced that nobody appreciated my efforts or understood my motivation, I never experienced disappointment or frustration overwhelming enough to ever seriously consider terminating early. On the contrary, I often surprised myself by how easily I adjusted to new surroundings and perplexing situations.

I became proficient at arguing with taxi drivers charging outrageous fares, but at the same time learned to be patient and accepting of circumstances that at home in New York I would have found intolerable. I learned to endure dealing with slow inefficient public servants with no sense of customer service. I can remember times of patiently waiting over an hour in an excruciatingly slow-moving queue to buy stamps at the post office. Generally, the casual and unhurried pace of life in the tropics suited me.

As months passed I adjusted to being surrounded by children nearly everywhere I went, all chanting "oyimbo, oyimbo," literally meaning "peeled one," the Yoruba way of addressing white strangers. I thought it an apt greeting, because the longer I lived in Africa the more I saw myself and other Caucasians as sickly-looking pale and anemic colorless corks bobbing about amidst a sea of dark and healthy looking bodies. Attention-getting crowds of children were especially large and energetic in remote locales, where the sight of a tall white man emerging from a yam-hauling lorry, or haggling over a loaf of bread or several tomatoes in a native market, were rare occurrences.

One day, thinking it would be good to have live animals in the biology classroom for the students to observe and enjoy, I went to a huge sprawling local native market to buy a guinea pig. Emerging from the taxi, I immediately attracted a group of children who followed behind me as I searched for the area in the vast market where live animals were sold. As I explored the market's maze of narrow aisles and passageways, I became a child magnet, attracting more and more children. They followed me down a long aisle lined by stalls selling chickens, then an aisle with goats, and finally to an area of closely packed market stalls selling only guinea pigs. I began walking down a long passage-way. There with hundreds of small stalls crowded together, each manned by a market woman selling live guinea pigs. Behind and following me were dozens of children excitedly jumping up and down, hoping for a handout, yelling "oyimbo." With curious market-goers and traders looking on, I thought myself the Pied Piper of Ibadan.

As I passed one stall after another, the market women held up fat squirming guinea pigs, smiling and laughing as they pointed out the prominent swollen scrotal sacs of the males. As the minutes passed, more children came running to join the others. My shopping trip soon deteriorated into a boisterous, chaotic scene. Pursued and surrounded by children, and with market women thrusting guinea pigs into my face at every turn, I beat a hasty guinea pig-less retreat and returned home. It was almost impossible to go shopping in an outdoor native market and remain anonymous and inconspicuous. Introvert that I was, both then and still now, I slowly adjusted to life in a goldfish bowl. Over time, I became less conscious of the crowds of children that followed me, the stares of curious by-standers, and the skin color of the Nigerians I moved among. Time assumed new meaning and I rarely looked at my watch. When it stopped working one day I gave up wearing a timepiece altogether.

Adjusting to new foods proved a relatively easy matter after the shock of our first in-country meal offering of boiled chicken heads, but I experienced a painful reminder that I wasn't in Kansas anymore when I was introduced to my first Nigerian home cooking.

Two months after arriving, one of my students, Godwin, invited me to his home for Sunday dinner. I looked forward to a home-cooked meal with some trepidation, a fear that was to prove well founded. I was eager to try new locally-prepared cuisine, and considered mild bouts of diarrhea an inconvenient, but tolerable, consequence. However, I was wary of the potential for more serious health risks, such as the possibility of parasitic infections like tapeworm and trichinosis associated with the ingestion of poorly cooked meat, or the possibility of water-borne diseases like amoebic dysentery. When a young girl began pouring water into the glass near my plate I thanked her, but told her that I preferred to drink hot tea at the end of the meal. My hosts may have boiled and filtered the water beforehand, but I was hesitant to inquire and possibly offend.

It was a large gathering of fourteen people, all seated at a single table with myself at one end. The meal consisted of bowls of "soup" for several persons to share, and two large communal bowls. One was filled with pounded yam ("fufu") and the other with ground cassava ("gari"), Nigeria's two carbohydrate-rich staples. I had tasted my first gari soon after arriving in Lagos. I found it similar to what I imagined eating course sawdust would be like, so I politely passed up the cassava and opted for the bowl of fufu, bearing a close resemblance to a mountain of mashed potatoes.

Following the lead of Godwin and others at the table, I left my chair and went to the communal bowl near the middle of the table containing the fufu minimountain, grabbed a handful, and returned to my seat. Observing others forming their fufu chunk into a bowl-like shape with their fingers, I did likewise. Once shaped, the fufu mass was immersed into the soup, crudely resembling tomato soup in which a few pieces of meat (likely goat or beef) were floating. Watching my dinner companions scoop their fufu through the soup and begin to eat, as I continued to clumsily fiddle with my fufu wad, I quickly discerned that one of the goals clearly seemed to be to snag one of the meat pieces along with the sauce. How observant and clever of me, I thought.

Since the meat supply was limited for so large a gathering, I decided to leave the meaty bits for others sitting near me. When I finally finished fashioning my large fufu mass into a cup that filled nearly my entire palm, I swished the fufu scoop through the soup, avoiding the meat chunks. My fufu cup filled to the brim with broth, I unhesitatingly stuffed the whole shebang into my mouth. More than anything else I wanted my hosts to feel that I enthusiastically appreciated their food and hospitality.

What followed was an absolute nightmare. Upon ingesting the fufu mass I experienced several minutes of sheer hell. I was in agony. I can still mentally picture the tableau of a Nigerian family at dinner, their faces all turned my way, showing mixed expressions ranging from astonishment to confused concern. Sitting there at the head of the table trying to catch my breath, willing myself not to leap and run from the room screaming in pain, I sat glued to my seat feeling like my throat was on fire.

Images flashed through my mind of pictures I recalled seeing in books, of torture scenes from the Spanish inquisition when hapless victims tied to tables with their mouths propped open endured the horror of having boiling water or molten gold poured down their throats. Now I knew how they must have felt.

The innocent looking soup was not soup at all, but the Devil's brew; a dynamite concoction laced with the hottest of hot peppers designed to test the mettle of any Peace Corps volunteer who dared to think they could come to dinner and remain inconspicuous after swallowing a soup-filled concavity of fufu.

Never in my life had I tasted anything so painfully hot. Minutes passed, as I sat gasping with chest heaving and eyes watering. Surely I had permanently scarred or irreparably damaged my esophagus. I would never eat again. I could visualize my obit in the Smithtown Messenger "Smithtown High graduate and naive PCV dies during meal in Africa after rashly swallowing fufu fire bomb."

After recovering to the point of finally being able to subnormally breath and speak, I remember uttering something trite about the spiciness of the soup. Then I gulped down all the water in my glass, with no thoughts about any pathogenic protozoa, microbes or spores it contained.

I can only conjecture how my hosts interpreted my violent reaction to the meal. My vision was still blurred by tearing eyes, and I could barely talk, when I bid them goodbye a short time later, after accepting their simple substitute offering of tea and toast. At school, Godwin never mentioned my dinner with his family and I was never invited back, so I'm guessing they found the incident nearly as painful as I did. I imagine, however, they had many laughs and entertaining stories to share with friends and neighbors, about the "oyimbo" that came to dinner and couldn't handle the soup.

7

The Days Drift Languidly by

Notwithstanding my early encounters with uniquely esoteric foods like boiled chicken heads, or challenging dishes like fiery hot pepper soup, I quickly learned to enjoy Nigerian cuisine, though never acquired a taste for gari or other cassava-based foods like eba or akpu.

Following my initial embarrassing encounter with pounded yam ("fufu"), I avoided it as well, though occasionally ate sliced boiled or fried yam ("dundun") served with vegetables.

In terms of food during my two years in Nigeria, I became a creature of habit. Breakfast consisted of either a bowl of fresh fruit, or hot tea with guinea fowl eggs scrambled with tomatoes and onions on toast. For supper I sometimes asked my cook-steward to stay and prepare me a special meal like hamburger and fried potatoes, rice with tomatoes and onions (joloff rice), curry, bean pie ("moin-moin"), or groundnut (peanut) stew. On most evenings, though, I fended for myself, and almost always ate what became, soon after my arrival in Ibadan, my favorite Nigerian food—bean cakes or "akara".

Akara, a common food in Yoruba speaking areas, is made from certain beans ground up in water to a creamy consistency. Onions and small hot peppers are added, and the cakes are then fried in peanut or palm oil. I discovered a woman living within a mile of my home who made absolutely delicious akara, using peanut oil and only a modest amount of hot peppers. Nearly every evening I trekked to her home to buy seven or eight of her freshly-made cakes. My nightly walk from Adeyoola Chambers, through crowded residential Oke-Badan neighborhoods to my akara woman, became an evening ritual.

She sat up shop in front of her home. When I arrived she was sitting on a wooden stool, surrounded by friends and family, including many children and a baby on her back. Around her were several bowls of liquefied beans, which she ladled into a large cauldron of hot peanut oil over a fire in front of her. After floating in the oil for several minutes, turned several times until crisp and brown,

37

she scooped up the cakes with a large metal slotted spoon that drained off excess oil. Then, smiling and thanking me, she handed me the cakes wrapped in sheets of newspaper, and I paid her two shillings. By the time I arrived home the paper was completely oil-soaked and the bean cakes still warm and ready for eating.

For two years, most evening meals consisted of akara cakes sandwiched between slices of bread, sausage rolls, and a quart bottle of Star beer. I never purchased food from the Western-style Kingsway store with all its amenities in the city, frequented by foreign expatriates, embassy personnel, or wealthy Nigerians. Instead, I preferred to buy from food stalls in my neighborhood, open air native markets, or from vendors who frequently came to my door, such as Mary the orange girl and Bose the guinea egg girl. Rarely did I need to fetch food, it nearly always came to me.

Because of my heavy teaching duties, I shared the house with a cook-steward who worked for me five days a week. He cleaned house, did laundry, bought some of my food in the market place, and prepared breakfast and sometimes dinner. I employed four cook-stewards during my time in Nigeria, starting with a young man named Mohammed. There were certain costs, among them a lack of privacy, associated with having another person roaming about the house, but these costs were significantly outweighed by the benefits. Had I attempted to buy food in the market I would have spent much time haggling over the price in accordance with the economic bartering system that prevailed, in addition to being overcharged for the food. Teaching duties demanded so much of my time and energy, that having someone at home to help with the laundry, shopping, cooking, and cleaning, was invaluable. I occasionally visited native markets on my own, but the novelty of having crowds of children swarming around me wherever I went, and the time-consuming hassles associated with bartering, quickly wore thin. When traveling or otherwise away from Adeyoola Chambers, I often purchased food from unfamiliar local vendors, a practice which compromised my health. However, I had decided before ever arriving in Africa that I was going to experience Nigeria in a total and intimate way, not as a foreigner from the outside looking, but not living, in.

There were two favorite vendors that I frequently patronized. Mrs. Idowu had a small wooden stand on the side of Liberty Stadium road about fifty yards from Adeyoola Chambers. I visited her weekly to buy sausage rolls, bread, tomatoes, and onions, and to select from the wide variety of imported goods on her shelves, like canned ham from the Netherlands or fruit preserves from Hungary. She always welcomed me with a broad smile, and we engaged in a long counter-exchange of greetings, oftentimes beginning from many yards away, as she first saw me leave the house and begin walking down the road towards her shop.

"Se, alafia ni," [hello] I began, as she looked towards me, observing my approach.

"A dupe," she called back in reply.

"Ile n ko?," [How is your house]. I continued.

"Eh," [OK] she replied.

"Omo re n ko?" [And your children]

"Eh."

The Yoruba have a highly elaborate system of greetings, one for nearly every occasion. The greeting ritual begins as soon as you see the person to be greeted, even if they are far away. No averting your head, pretending not to see, or looking away or down at your feet until you are nearly upon the person and then decide to finally make eye contact, as in our culture. Greeting an approaching person can be a long drawn out affair, and can continue on once you have passed one another.

The greeting ritual fascinated me, and at one point I memorized a lengthy Yoruba greeting for the highly specific occasion of "greeting someone you haven't seen for a very long time working in a yam field on a rainy day." The right opportunity to use the greeting never presented itself. One day, during the rainy season, I walked to a nearby yam plantation in pouring rain in hopes of being able to use the greeting, but I couldn't find anyone working in the field and returned home drenched.

I was a loyal customer of Mrs. Idowu for two years. My steady business likely provided her the income needed to pay a goodly portion of her children's school fees. I was continually amazed by the variety of products she offered for sale, and how many cans and boxes she was able to display on the shelves of her little roadside shack, measuring only about twelve square feet. Once I bought a small jar of Hellmann's mayonnaise, a rare find.

The other shop owner I visited often was a younger woman named Beatrice. She had a small shop with food and household provisions located a fifteen minute walk away. Beatrice reminded me of Thoreau's quote about those among us who live lives of quiet desperation. She had seven young children, all girls, and was desperate to produce a son to please her husband and, presumably, to fulfill lagging feelings of personal self-worth.

A woman's prestige in Yorubaland is insidiously tied to how many babies, especially males, she can bear and raise. Women unable to produce sons are considered failures by husbands who have no understanding of the basis for human sex determination, and who fail to realize that if anyone is to blame for an embryo's sex chromosome complement it is they, not their wives. As I became better acquainted with Beatrice, I realized how sad and hopeless a life she led. I never did meet her husband. It was probably best that I didn't. Had I done so, I might have said something rash like "What's the matter, can't you make any Y-bearing sperm to ease your poor wife's suffering?"

Beatrice dressed in the style typical of Yoruba women, wearing a blouse-like top with a high neckline ("buba"), and a length of fabric called a wrapper ("iro"), wrapped around and tucked in at the waist. For the entire time I knew her she carried an infant on her back, a form of maternal care common in Africa that ensures security, warmth, and close bodily contact between mother and infant. A length of cloth tied under mother's armpits secures the infant's torso and neck, and a sash securing the baby's backside is well tied so the infant cannot fall.

Among Beatrice's brood were a pair of twins. Yoruba women have one of the highest twinning rates in the world, about forty-five twins in every one thousand births. The first born twin, whether a boy or girl, is always named Taiwo ("having the first taste of the world"), and the second twin is always given the name Kehinde ("arriving after the other"). Interestingly, the Yoruba consider Taiwo, the first born, as the younger twin, sent into the outside world by the more senior twin Kehinde to check things out. When the more curious and adventuresome Taiwo signals the coast is clear by crying, the more intelligent and reflective Kehinde follows. Because of relatively high infant mortality rates, and lack of medical and early maternal care in Africa generally, many twins die soon after birth.

Among the Yoruba in historically recent times an interesting practice and belief system has arisen involving the birth of twins, viewed as an omen of good fortune for the family. The Yoruba believe twins share the same combined soul, and should one or both of the twins die the soul of the deceased must be appeased. As part of the cultural grieving process a wooden carving of the lost child is commissioned by the parents with the guidance of a diviner, a Babalowo, who helps the parents select the artist who will do the work. If both twins die, two figures are carved. The carvings or effigies are called Ere ibeji (ere = sacred image, ibi = born, eji = two).

During one of my visits, Beatrice told me of an elderly woman who needed money and was looking for someone to purchase a pair of ibeji that she had cared for and owned for many years. The following week, I visited Beatrice's shop to meet the woman. She arrived alone, carrying a well worn cloth bag. She was elderly and walked slowly with a stoop. Her clothing was faded and frayed, her face deeply lined. It was obvious to me that her life had been hard. After Beatrice introduced her to me speaking Yoruba, the woman opened her bag and removed two lumps of cloth; she slowly and carefully unwrapped each to reveal a set of ibeji twins, a male and a female.

The carvings were ten inches tall and portrayed figures on pedestals, standing with hands on hips. They appeared to be quite old. They were carved from a light brown wood, and showed adult anatomical features typical of ibeji: defined pubic hair and adult genitalia. The anatomical proportions were not to scale. The head and torso were disproportionately larger than the legs, the massive shoulders and upper arms twice as wide as the hips. Both ibeji had a belt of yellow beads around the waist, and a bracelet of green and brown beads on the left wrist. Each had different beaded bracelets on the right wrist. Around the elongated neck of each carving was a beaded necklace; on the male twin it consisted of alternating green and yellow beads. Both figures showed the same pattern of pronounced facial scarification, with three short vertical scars on both upper cheeks. Below these, four longer horizontal scars extended most of the length of the face. In both carvings the pupils of the eyes were represented by short metal nails pounded into the wood. The carvings were smooth and well worn, suggesting frequent handling from ritual use in the past. Perhaps, as is often the case, the woman had handled the carvings as she danced with them or sang to them.

Except for the gender differences, the two carvings were so similar it was obvious that they had been made by the same wood carver, and represented a pair of fraternal twins that had died at birth or in early infancy. From the attitude and expressions of the old woman I adjudged her to be sincere when she told me, through Beatrice as interpreter, that she desperately needed money, and hoped that I would buy her ibejis. From the delicate care she showed in packing and gently handling the carvings, I could tell they were treasured possessions whose absence would be missed. I made no effort to barter with her, and paid her initial asking price. I cannot remember how much I paid for the carvings, but am certain that it was too little. This is the sad circumstance of how I came to own the first of two sets of ibeji carvings acquired during my time in Yorubaland.

Frequently Nigerians asked me why I had not married or fathered children. On several occasions I received marriage proposals from concerned friends, acquaintances, even strangers, who brought marriageable young women to my home. I always attempted to casually skirt discussions of personal matters like marriage or family, but, curiously, I talked about such things with Beatrice, even though we were nearly strangers. It was as if we sensed ourselves sympathetic kindred spirits.

Several days before departing Nigeria, I visited her shop to tell her that I would soon be leaving, to say my goodbyes and wish her well. On that occasion we visited for over an hour. She talked candidly to me of her predicament, and how she despaired her condition of perpetual pregnancy and her large family. I remember the poignancy of our last meeting and how, surrounded by her seven girls and well advanced in another pregnancy, she looked so tired and old beyond her years. As I turned away to leave her shop I heard her lamenting "Too many, too many," the last words she spoke to me.

When I arrived in Nigeria in May of 1964 it was a country with a population of about fifty-six million people. The total fertility rate (TFR) was 6.9, meaning that the average Nigerian woman would bear 6.9 children during the child-bearing years of her reproductive lifetime. The average woman! Beatrice, with seven young girls and another baby on the way, was destined to be one of many Nigerian women to exceed the country's TFR. How many of these women, like Beatrice, desired a life free of the reproductive servitude of continual child-bearing and child-rearing? How many, like Beatrice, wanted a life affording them some control over their personal reproductive lives and destiny?

Shortly after purchasing the ibeji carvings from the elderly woman in Beatrice's shop, I visited a small village on the outskirts of Ibadan, and another aged woman approached me and beckoned me to enter her simple hut. Once inside, she showed me a wood carving that she urged me to buy. At the time I did not fully understand the significance of the carving, but she was insistent that I buy it. Once again, I paid her initial asking price, making no attempt to barter lower. Like the ibejis, this carving was old and worth much more than I paid for it. In the traditional Yoruba religious belief system there is a supreme deity (Olurun) and a pantheon of lesser deities (Orishas), one of which is Shango, the god of thunder and lightening. The wood carving I purchased, I later learned, was a representation of Shango, as the figure carried atop its head a double axe, the emblem of Shango. It is perhaps no coincidence that the Yoruba worship a thunder god when one considers that the area of West Africa where they live has one of the highest frequencies of thunderstorms anywhere in the world, exceeded only by Java.

In Africa I adjusted to eating only two meals a day, with occasional snacks at lunchtime, a policy I continue to this day. Supper was my big meal of the day, and if it wasn't akara it was often beans in some other form. Rice and beans, a staple in many 3rd world countries, is an excellent meatless meal of complimentary plant proteins. Beans are high in the amino acids that are deficient in rice, and vice versa. Favorite rice meals included curried rice or joloff rice, cooked with tomato sauce, tomatoes, onions and meat, or rice with fried plantain, cooked in palm or peanut oil. Fried plantain, like akara, was a favorite food, and after work I often purchased some from a native vendor. She sat up her shop underneath the banana trees next to my back door, or by my motorbike shed on Liberty Stadium Road. For six pence she gave me several slices of fried plantain ("dodo"), wrapped in banana leaves.

I refused to fret about the cleanliness of the leaves or the vendor, or of the quality of the water she used to wash the leaves. Had I done so I know I would not have enjoyed nearly as well the taste of the plantain. I refused to overly worry about getting sick or picking up nematode worm infections, figuring that even the most cautious and non-adventuresome were bound to sicken or get a few worms. Although wary of more serious worm infections from poorly cooked meat, such as tapeworms, I generally relaxed and enjoyed native foods; not an intelligent strategy, but I do know that I enjoyed African food and spent little time fretting over my health.

In this regard I think specifically of friends Ed and Helen, the Peace Corps couple living below me. They were fastidious and conscientious, zealously refusing food from native vendors, always taking packed lunches with them when they traveled. They assiduously ate only those fruits that had a natural protective peelable cover, like bananas and oranges, and only those leafy vegetables that had been soaked at least fifteen minutes in a Clorox solution. In spite of all their precautions, examination of their stool samples at their final medical check showed they were filled with worms.

One day I had a craving for a hamburger, and asked Mohammed to make me one. I was awakened early the next morning by loud banging noises. It sounded like someone was breaking down the outside door, or using a sledgehammer to knock a hole in a wall. Thinking the noise temporary and from workmen in the neighborhood, I remained in bed, but the pounding went on and on. Finally I got out of bed and investigated. The racket was coming from my kitchen. Mohammed had returned from market with a slab of beef that he was diligently tenderizing on the kitchen floor, relentlessly pulverizing it with a wooden mallet. Meat bought in the native market had to be treated thusly he assured me, else it would be too tough. Subsequent attempts to eat meat not so persistently brutalized convinced me he was right.

At that time most of the cattle in tropical southern Nigeria were herded down from the more arid north, where livestock were less plagued by wasting diseases such as sleeping sickness transmitted by Tsetse flies. Because the cow that contributed the hunk of meat Mohammed was so energetically pounding on my kitchen floor had been slaughtered in an Ibadan meat market after walking about five hundred miles from the sub-Sahara, the meat was understandably tough. Knowing how time consuming and energy-demanding a hamburger was to prepare, I took pity on Mohammed and my ear drums, and rarely requested one thereafter.

If I got hungry at school I ate a banana or some peanuts, a handful of which could be purchased from vendors visiting the staff room for only three pence. Sometimes I snacked on a peanut/popcorn mixture, always an interesting undertaking because the native vendors popped the corn kernels in hot sand. Eating popcorn laced with sand grains was uncomfortable in the mouth and brutal on tooth enamel, but may have had a bonus effect of an intestinal scouring action.

A favorite snack in the evening before bed was a large bowl of fresh fruit that my cook/steward prepared and put in the frig to chill before leaving for the day. I remember those wonderfully indulgent feelings late at night, after working several hours on lesson plans or grading papers. I relaxed on the couch, listening to night-calling frogs or insects, or the sound of rain falling on the metal roof, watching the geckos running along the walls and ceiling, snapping up mosquitoes and other insects, while I ate a bowl of fresh tropical salad made from banana, pineapple, oranges, grapefruit, mango and papaya.

Cassava

Gari, a staple food in Nigeria, is made from cassava tubers that are peeled and then ground. The ground cassava is dried in the sun, or pressed with stone slabs for several days, to remove moisture, and then baked over an open fire. Cassava is carbohydrate-rich and protein-poor. It supplies needed energy, but lacks the amino acids needed for tissue growth and cell repair.

As I traveled in Nigeria it was common to see large areas roadside covered by drying cassava, and not uncommon to see children afflicted with Kwashiorkor, a condition of malnourishment. In spite of brittle hair and nails and some skin bleaching, Kwashiorkor sufferers can appear deceptively healthy because of their noticeably swollen bellies, but the bloated abdomens are symptoms of edema associated with protein starvation, not because of full stomachs. Children fed a largely yam or cassava based diet receive adequate calories, but lack the proteins especially needed by young growing bodies. Throughout West Africa, cassava was in plentiful supply and inexpensive to purchase.

Yoruba ibeji carvings

The cultural traditions and beliefs relating to newborn mortality in twins among the Yoruba reflects a unique and fascinating ritualization of the bereavement process. Even more curious is the fact that although the ibeji represents a dead newborn, the carving is in the form of a mature human, with well defined adult features of large breasts, pubic hair, mature coiffures often colored with blue or indigo dye, gender specific facial scarification, and adult genitalia. Female ibeji may have super-sized pointed breasts, and can exude an erotic sexuality. When the ibeji carving(s) are completed the artist is given a feast and payment, and the carving(s) are brought to the household and cared for by the mother and female family members, or later on by the surviving twin or other relatives. Ibeji are treated reverently and as though they were alive, rubbed in oil, sung and prayed to, and often decorated with metal, beadwork, or cowrie shells. The carvings can remain in a family for generations.

Nigeria's population explosion

A high TFR is a major contributing factor to a countries population growth. Census data for African countries like Nigeria is typically imperfect and incomplete, but today (in 2007) Nigeria's population is estimated to be around 130 million, a significant increase from the population of fifty-six million in 1964. Today, Nigeria is the 8th or 9th most populated country in the world, and home to about one in every five Africans. Although by 2007 the TRF had declined from about 6.9 to 5.5, this number is still much too high as the infrastructure of the country cannot cope with such explosive growth in numbers of people.

Although women in Nigeria are having fewer numbers of children than their mothers did, as evidenced by the declining TFR, there are so many more women having those fewer numbers of children, that the population is still rapidly growing. Given the fact that about half of all Nigerians are under the age of fifteen, there is little hope of slowing this built-in momentum for further accelerated growth. It is projected that by the year 2050, Nigeria will be the worlds 4th most populous country, with about three hundred million inhabitants. The consequences of uncontrolled human numbers on a finite planet are insidious, and with widespread ripple effects, including destruction and degradation of natural habitats, pollution, and loss of wildlife resources. Human pressures on wildlife is especially significant in highly populated Nigeria, and especially in non-urban areas, where bushmeat is an important dietary component of rural Nigerians.

Presently the average Nigerian has to try to exist on about $1/day. There are scores of unemployed young people with nothing to do but be idle or get into trouble. People need shelter, clean water, balanced and adequate diets, a job that gives them enough money to live, and a sense of personal satisfaction that allows them to face each new day with some sense of optimism. People need a decent education that challenges their mind, proper health care, and the opportunity to hope for a life that could be considered meaningful. How can this happen in a rapidly growing country like Nigeria? How dense can Nigeria get? How dense can the world get, before humanity begins working towards a future premised on the quality of life rather than its quantity?

8

The Barber Arrives—
a Hair-lowering Experience

In August 1964, several months after arriving in Nigeria, I realized I needed a haircut. I asked Mohammed if he knew of a local barber. He told me that he knew of an itinerant barber who periodically visited the neighborhood. When I asked him if the man knew how to cut the hair of Europeans he answered that he wasn't sure, but that he would find the man, and I could ask him myself. I told Mohammed that I wanted a local barber, a traditional barber, someone that the other men in the neighborhood used. I felt strongly about this matter. I wanted what limited money I spent to patronize the tradesmen used by my Nigerian neighbors, to go directly into the local native economy.

The next weekend, on a Saturday morning, the barber arrived. He was an older man dressed in traditional costume, in his late 40's or 50's. From his facial scars I adjudged him to be a Yoruba man, and he spoke reasonably good pidgin English. I asked him several questions to ascertain the level of his comprehension, as I wanted to be sure he understood my instructions for the haircut. His white dashiki was well worn, frayed, and noticeably soiled. He had a cloth sack over his shoulder. In his hand he carried a large weather-beaten black leather bag with a clasp and handles, much like a country doctor.

"Can you do the hair of Europeans?" I asked.

"Oh, yes sir," he replied.

"Have you cut the hair of Europeans before?"

"Oh, yes sir," he repeated, draping my body with a soiled white sheet removed from his sack.

"Are you certain you can cut my hair, give me a good haircut?"

"Yes sir, very good haircut sir."

In hesitant fashion he briefly touched my hair, then opened his leather bag revealing antique-looking barbering instruments. Some were old and rusted, looking like they might have come from a museum collection. There were several pairs of scissors, several unusually large, and a wicked pair of black shears that resembled hedge trimmers. First he removed a pair of scissors and a large metal comb. Then he pulled from the bag some metal electric clippers, the dull steel head covered with rust patches, and plugged them into the outlet by the kitchen table where I was sitting. He seemed nervous, his movements awkward and tentative, but I assumed this was because we had first met, he was working in unfamiliar surroundings, and dealing with a "European" much larger and taller than himself. He spoke a few words in Yoruba to Mohammed, hovering in the background, then began making tentative and periodic single cuts with the scissors.

Snip ... (pause) ... snip ... (pause) ... as he moved back and forth around me. The day was hot and sultry, and I settled back in one of my two straight-backed wooden kitchen chairs. I sat away from the table, facing the open back door, occasionally gazing out at my yard and the dirt road leading up the hill to surrounding houses in my crowded neighborhood. Through the doorway, I saw a constant procession of people walking up and down the road, engaged in their chores and daily activities. Groups of barefoot children were carrying heavy metal pails of water on their heads, holding them steady with one hand to minimize spillage. Women were calling out and carrying their wares in baskets, trays, or boxes expertly balanced on their heads: oranges, mangos, plantains, eggs, plastic ballpoint pens and cigarette lighters, cigarettes, puff puff pastries, or chewing sticks.

I could see the section of my back yard containing a small grove of bananas, a bougainvillea with purple blossoms, hibiscus bushes with red or yellow flowers, and four papaya trees with clusters of unripe green papayas framed against the blue sky.

I relaxed in the chair, enjoying a slight breeze that came through the open door, passing through the living room and out the balcony door beyond. In a somnambulant state, I closed my eyes, paying little attention to the sounds of the barbering instruments and the barber hovering above me. He was now using the clippers. The whirring sound reminding me of the cicadas back in Illinois. It could only have been a minute or two, when the sensation of feeling clumps of long hair strands cascading down my face broke my languid reverie. I opened my eyes just as a big hunk of falling hair brushed my eyebrows. I glanced down at the sheet covering my lap in disbelief. There was a pile of hair there.

Where were all those long lengths of hair coming from? The clippers whirred away, positioned just above my forehead. Good God, were those hair hunks the amputated remains of my widow's peak? When it finally dawned on me what was likely happening, shocked from my torpor, I yelled for the barber to stop. Throwing off the hair-covered sheet, I dashed into the bathroom to look at myself in the mirror. Surprise, horror. The mirror didn't lie. The entire front one-third of my head had been scalped. I looked like a Hare Krishna.

I rushed out of the bathroom, yelling at the barber that the haircut was finished, paid him several shillings, and quickly sent him away. As he was hastily packing up his implements, he excitedly conversed in Yoruba with Mohammed. They were both caught off guard by the unexpected dramatic turn of events, likely wondering about the sudden fit that had come over the "oyimbo."

From my near-hysterical reaction they must have thought me mad, but I was more shocked than angry. It took over a month for my hair to resume some state of normalcy. From then on, I went to the barber shop near the Kingsway store in the city for my haircuts. The barbers there catered to a special clientele: U.S. and British embassy officials and AID personnel. The decision to pay for the services of high-priced barbers that almost exclusively served Caucasians was the one concession I made during my two years in Africa to not embrace the traditional culture and economy.

Weeks later, sometime in September, I caught Mohammed stealing the two blue dress shirts I brought with me from America, but never worn. Reluctantly, I dismissed him. He was followed by my second cook-steward Daniel, who worked for me for several months until personal family matters forced him to leave Ibadan. He was replaced by diligent and hard-working Moses. He never caused any problems, was a wonderful cook, and worked for me for over a year, but I was forced to fire him after a series of troubling theft incidents. By that time, friends Ed and Helen were making preparations to leave the country, and I inherited their honest and conscientious cook-steward Joshua, who worked for me during my last four months in Nigeria.

9

Hail Sinner!—I Go to Church

On November 8, 1964, I attended church for the first time since arriving in Ibadan. I was invited by relatives of one of my biology students to be one of several special participants in a Sunday service at The Blessed Church of Christ (Ijo Ibukun Ti Kristi) in the Oke-Ado area of the city. The day was lovely, and passers-by returned the few Yoruba phrases of greeting I knew with their own greetings and smiles, as I sauntered along Liberty Stadium Road in full Nigerian dress from Adeyoola Chambers to the church, a forty-five minute walk. It was the church's big event of the year, a festive harvest celebration. Seven special guests from Ibadan had been invited to participate—Mr. Amusan, a general trader; Mr. Adekoya, an accountant; Mr. Shogbesan, an insurance broker; Mr. Ayoola, a solicitor; Chief Ogunlesi, the Director of Broadway Printers; Mr. Olomo, a politician from the Ibadan Ministry of Finance; and me, tutor at IBHS.

The program for the occasion was detailed in a small nineteen page booklet with a pink cover. It consisted of songs and spoken passages. At the beginning of the service, to the accompaniment of joyous singing and hand-clapping, as befits a harvest celebration, all seven of us marched in single file, I at the end of the procession, and took our designated seats on a raised dais facing the congregation. The church was packed, about two hundred people. I was the only Caucasian in the room, and had worn a brand new traditional Nigerian outfit made especially for the occasion. One of my students, Musa, had introduced me to an honest, hard-working tailor in the city. He had made me a beautiful traditional Yoruba man's outfit. It consisted of a flowing outer garment, a sapara (agbada), worn over a matching shirt (orbuba) and trousers (sokoto). All were made of cloth with alternating narrow blue and white stripes. The sokoto, tightened with a drawstring, closely resembled pajama bottoms. On my head, I wore an attractive felt tan and beige patterned fila.

The service was long, lasting about two hours. As the morning festivities wore on the church increasingly approached sauna-like conditions. Midway in the service each special guest was recognized in turn. All seven of us were listed in the program, each with a full page devoted to us, including a special song in our honor. The six Nigerian honorees had songs in Yoruba. I was listed last, and my song was in English—"The harvest is passing, the summer will end." My song began with the phrase "Hark sinner while God from on high doth entreat thee," a curious coincidence, as I was certain none of the program planners knew I was an agnostic and infrequent churchgoer.

Growing up in Smithtown, my main reason for faithfully attending the First Presbyterian Church on Main Street each Sunday, was because I enjoyed singing in the choir under the direction of choir master Don Gardner. Mr. Gardner wrote several pieces of religious music including *"Man does not live by bread alone,"* which the choir often sang at Sunday services, but was best known for the song *"All I want for Christmas is my two front teeth,"* a ditty he dashed off one evening, while enjoying the company of his incisor-less granddaughter.

I had absolutely no idea what to expect during the church service. I had come only because it seemed unfriendly to turn down the original invitation. All I had been told was that it was a harvest celebration, that the congregation would be honored by my attendance, and that I was expected to bring a donation. No one had bothered to mention that it was a highly publicized special church occasion, or that the other honorees included important local officials, successful business-men, and well-off politicians.

I had a ten pound note in my trouser pocket, at that time equivalent to about $24.00. I had given some thought to my donation. I wanted to be generous and let the congregation know how much I appreciated the honor of being asked to participate. But I didn't want to embarrass the other participants and project myself as a fat cat, filthy rich American; $24.00 amounted to nearly a week's worth of my modest Peace Corps subsistence allowance.

As I sat on stage with the other honorees, I began to wish I had brought some one and five pound notes in the event that I decided to reduce the amount of my donation during the service. Looking out over the congregation, I began to have concerns and reservations. Would they interpret my ten pound donation as excessive, perhaps even offensive? Was I about to project a blatant and unneces-sary show of wealthy American arrogance? Too late now, I'm here, and all I have with me is the single ten pound note.

After nearly an hour spent reciting religious passages and singing eight anthems, many of them with multiple stanzas and long solo parts, the special part of the ceremony began. The choir and full church congregation stood up and began to sing "Omo Arowosola ti nro bi ojo …" Mr. Amusan, the general trader, proudly arose from his seat, and began dancing. Aha, so dancing is part of the ritual. Well, I can handle that, I thought.

He danced slowly and gracefully, keeping rhythm with the music's beat, to a box located off to the side of the stage. I hadn't been aware of the box until then. Arriving at the box he reached into his pocket, deposited something inside, then shuffled back to his seat, keeping beat with the music all the way. As he was returning to his seat, an elegantly dressed Nigerian woman standing by the collection box, who had been singing some of the solo vocal parts throughout the service, reached into the box and held up the offering for all the congregation to see. "Twenty pounds," she announced. The congregation responded with cheers and shouts of approval. Mr. Amusan smiled, faced the audience, graciously received their praise, then took his seat. Good grief, I thought.

Then it was the turn of Mr. Adekoya, the accountant. A soloist began singing the first verse of his specially selected song "F'Olunun wa o Olorun Ibukun iba Re to to, K'a to korin o ajuba Emi Mimo …" Several portly older women from the congregation left their seats and moved into the center aisle of the church, singing and shaking, as Mr. Adekoya danced across the floor to the money box. In slow, subdued fashion he glided gracefully across the stage. Nearing the box he picked up the tempo, showing off some special dancing skills. Then, finishing with a flourish involving several twirls of his body, he stuck his hand in the box. "Twenty pounds," the box keeper announced, holding up and waving about a crisp twenty pound note for all to see. More cheers from the congregation.

The insurance broker and the solicitor were even more generous. Sitting on stage watching their performances, facing the multitude, I was feeling sick to my stomach and increasingly uncomfortable. Rivers of perspiration poured from my armpits. My hands were clammy. I sensed the blood draining from my face, my clothes becoming damp and clinging.

Then Chief Ogunlesi took to the floor in his elegant traditional dress. Exhibiting fancy footwork, he danced across the stage and really upped the ante. "Fifty pounds," the woman announced to the congregation, which responded enthusiastically with joyous shouting and clapping. I sat motionless and stone-faced. The seat of my sokoto was sopping wet. When I shifted slightly I could feel the back of my sapara plastered with perspiration to the back of my chair. What had I gotten myself into? Could this be really happening? Or was it all a bad dream, related somehow to last evening's meal of highly seasoned curry?

Then it was Mr. Olomo's turn. Looking at his elegant apparel, a beautiful white sapara with elaborate embroidery and gold braid, I had a gut feeling that he was going to surpass everyone, duly impressing all assembled with his generosity.

I was not disappointed. Rising almost triumphantly from his seat, he immediately pulled from his pocket a crisp new one hundred pound note, which he held up and waved above his head as he began to dance across the stage. The consummate politician, he obviously intended to make the most of his opportunity to play to a full house.

His dance was lengthy and over-the-top. There were elaborate embellishments: body twirls, arm and leg extensions, and knee bends with crouching that brought his body close to the floor. As he danced, he kept waving the hand holding the note. Pleased with the size of his donation, he put on a terrific show. The congregation went wild.

At the end of his performance I felt about as big as a microbe, or one of the suspended dust motes visible in the beams of light streaming into the church through the stained glass windows. Had the floor opened up and swallowed me from view, I would have been thankful. Good Lord, had someone deliberately arranged the program honorees in the order of presumed wealth and anticipated size of gift giving? Nearly every participant preceding me had made a contribution an order of magnitude greater than the one previous. Did these folks think I was a Rockefeller? Didn't they know I was a helplessly middle class American, subsisting on a Peace Corps living allowance of less than $5/day?

I yearned to be delivered from my impending embarrassment. Let this agony be over quickly. Why hadn't someone told me about the nature of the harvest celebration, the gift-giving obligation of the honorees, the magnitude of gifts commonly given? Why had they placed me last on the list of potential donors? I was about to be humiliated in front of two hundred people. The women's chorus began to sing "Hark sinner while God from on high doth entreat thee …"

Everyone was on their feet, smiling, swaying, and hand clapping. Mr. Olomu and the others all turned their heads in my direction. It all seemed like a bad dream. I slowly rose up from my chair, all eyes on me, and started to move with the music, the seat of my sokoto and my orbuba darkened by perspiration.

"And warning with accents of mercy doth blend …"

My clothes were plastered to my body. Had I just stepped from a sauna, I couldn't imagine looking any more bedraggled. The rim of my fila was wet. Sweat coursed down my face, as I sensed myself anemically and inelegantly shuffling towards the insidious box and the fated announcement. I didn't want my dance to be anti-climatic following the politician's energetic performance, but I had no enthusiasm, no joie de vivre, as I sensed myself creeping along like an amoeba with an iron deficiency. I felt like an Arthur Murray reject, that my life force had left me.

"Give ear to His voice lest in judgment he meet thee ..."

I imagined what everyone was thinking, sitting on the edges of their seats. "What's he going to do to top Mr. Olomo?" I could imagine all the pent up energy ready to be vented in cheers and shouts at the announcement. "Two hundred pounds from the American tutor!" My song seemed to go on forever. The previous participants had measured their dancing so that their arrival at the box and the return trip to their seats coincided with the length of their song. Had they practiced beforehand? The trip to and from the collection box couldn't be more than thirty feet, but I felt like I was moving in slow motion. Oh God, let their be some sudden event to distract the congregation. A sudden storm, perhaps. A massive thunderbolt. Let their be a miracle. A total solar eclipse, that blackens the church. Let this ghastly day be over.

"The harvest is passing, the summer will end."

I turned and looked out at the congregation. The atmosphere inside the church was fever pitch, everyone standing, hands clapping and bodies swaying, all primed for the climax of festivities, the reservoir release of all the accumulated pent up energy, the shouts of joy and jubilation. I reached the accursed box at a point about midway in the song, deposited the soggy crumpled ten pound note that I had clutched in my clammy hand for what had seemed like an eternity, and began the long dance back to my seat. Agony, misery. I wanted to run back to the seat, to have my moment of ignominy end quickly. But what then? I would be sitting in my chair facing the congregation while the choir was still on the third verse, with the final verse yet to come. Better I keep moving, even if it seemed like I was maneuvering through thick molasses.

Soon after I dropped the sweat-dampened wadded note in the collection box, and was nearing the security of my seat, I heard the woman announce "Ten pounds." The silence in the church was oppressive ... soon followed by what agonizingly sounded like a few audible gasps ... then feeble polite applause. Mercifully, the service concluded soon after.

I stayed briefly at the reception following, watching members of the congregation besiege Mr. Olomo, gushing over the magnitude of his Christian charity. He looked really pleased with himself. After the obligatory polite niceties, I slowly moved towards the door, nodding to people as I passed, and beat a hasty retreat. That was my first and last appearance at the Blessed Church of Christ. They say that religion comforts. Not so for me that day.

10

Sundays Are Special

In Nigeria, as in West Africa generally, Sundays are special. People stroll about the streets in their best clothes, stopping in to visit friends, often unannounced and unexpectedly. I was never certain who would show up on my doorstep on a Sunday, but someone usually did. To prepare for guests, I always had the frig stocked with quart bottles of Star beer, Fanta, and a gourd filled with palm wine ("emu"), delivered weekly by a young man on a bicycle. Babatunde, my palm wine tapper, was my steady supplier for all of my two years at Adeyoola Chambers. Reliable people told me that he was trustworthy, and didn't dilute his wine with river water containing potentially hazardous microbes. Early on Saturday mornings I awaited his knock on my back door. When I opened it, there was Babatunde with my palm wine, the open top of the gourd covered by a banana leaf securely tied down with string.

To satisfy the hunger of visitors I kept a cache of sausage rolls, some groundnuts (peanuts), fruit, and cold bean cakes. On Sundays, students, friends, people I barely knew, and sometimes total strangers, visited. Often a group of talking drummers appeared and began drumming below my balcony. In response, I left the house dressed in my usual weekend attire of dashiki, white shorts and tire sandals, and danced out into the street to greet them, thanking them for their visit by placing schilling coins on their sweaty foreheads. My antics always drew a crowd of amused on-lookers.

One Sunday evening, I heard knocking on my door as I sat at my desk preparing for school the next day. Opening the door, I saw a middle-aged Nigerian couple I had never seen before. They introduced themselves as the aunt and uncle of Akintunde, one of my students at IBHS. I invited them inside, and offered them orange Fanta and a bowl of groundnuts. He was in a business suit, she in elegant traditional dress. Her wrapper was made of expensive cloth of alternating broad blue and white stripes. On her head, she wore a beautiful headpiece made from fabric with a golden metallic quality. We engaged in small talk for a while, and

55

then the woman initiated a series of probing questions. "How do you like work at the school?" "Do you like Nigerian people?" "How do you find the food?"

After a series of conventional queries the woman finally broached the subject that I anticipated was coming, and assumed was the intended purpose of their visit. She moved her head, slowly scanning my living room, then looked at me and spoke.

"You have no wife, no children?"

"No," I answered, "I am not yet ready to marry."

They shook their heads imperceptibly, indicating sympathy at my wifeless plight. After all, the major purpose in life, the major joy in living, was to produce children, wasn't it? And for this a wife is useful.

"It is not good to live alone. It would be good for you to have a wife," she continued.

"It is not yet time," I said. "I'm still trying to figure out who I am. I'm not ready to try to figure out how to learn to live with someone else."

This seemed to puzzle them. As well it might. After all, what has knowing someone else got to do with marriage and family? I could see where the conversation was heading. During my stay in Nigeria I received several marriage proposals, all offered with the best of intentions, I'm sure. Why choose to live alone, when you could live in fruitful union, bearing children to be your legacy and support in old age?

"It is too bad you are not married. There are many eligible girls."

Although my intended mate remained anonymous, I assumed that the couple had a particular girl in mind, perhaps their daughter or a niece. Whenever the subject of my unmarried status came up in conversation, I always tried to handle the matter with good humor and quick dispatch. I had memorized a saying in Yoruba. Translated, it implied that "I have not yet met the woman who could satisfy me." I have since forgotten the actual phrase, but it went something like: "Eyo re to a ti ni o wu mi."

Yoruba is a tonal language, with no words generally longer than six letters. The alphabet is similar to that of English, with several notable omissions such as letters C, Q, X, and Z. Because the language is tonal, the meaning of a word can vary according to the inflection. For example, by way of an imaginary illustration: the word "mi" could mean either "me," "go," "love," "dirty," "harlot," or "stewpot," depending on whether it was spoken low, high, with an upward inflection, a downward inflection, etc. I found Yoruba a difficult language to master, and I rarely used it, as most Nigerians spoke either the Queen's English or pidgin English.

So, when I told the woman that I had not yet found the woman to satisfy me (or thought I had), she laughed heartily, and we left the matter of marriage and moved on to talking about other things. My stock reply in response to questions about wife and marriage almost always got a laugh. I assumed it was because Yoruba people accepted the bluntness of my reply, but, of course, it may have been because I botched my pronunciation and told them "I sleep fitfully only on happy mangos," or something equally absurd.

It was a warm June evening, the beginning of the rainy season, and the woman was sitting in a chair underneath the only wall lamp in my living room. The lamp, consisting of a bright incandescent bulb and a wicker shade, was located adjacent to the door opening to my balcony overlooking Stadium Road, a heavily traveled road leading to Liberty Stadium, Ibadan's major soccer venue, about a mile away. There was a cool evening breeze coming through the open door. Many insects had proliferated as a result of recent rains. The insects flew into the living room where they were pursued by my resident gecko's, scampering over the walls and ceiling. With the exception of mosquitoes, vectors for the malarial parasite, I was unconcerned about insects or other creepy crawlies, as most house invaders quickly fell prey to the patrolling geckos. I enjoyed watching their antics, and listening to their barking vocalizations. Also, as an amateur entomologist, I was interested in tropical insects, and in seeing what kinds entered the house from the surrounding neighborhood.

Among the insects out that evening were numerous large "sausage-flies," actually winged female termites with large egg-swollen abdomens. The rains had stimulated them to disperse en masse from their home colonies, instinctively seeking to reproduce and start new nests elsewhere. They entered the open door and flew to the light, fluttered about briefly, then shed their wings, and dropped to the floor.

As we were conversing, the women reached down to the floor, picked up the wiggling wingless insects, and popped them in her mouth. Her movements were relaxed and casual, as if eating a downed sausage-fly was no big deal, the most natural thing in the world. When it first happened I watched in stunned silence, hoping my facial expression didn't give me away. But as the evening progressed, and several dozen consumed insects later, her behavior impressed me as natural and utilitarian. Why disrupt social intercourse with friends by excusing yourself to go to the kitchen for snacks, when nutritious protein-rich tidbits are dropping right at your feet like manna from heaven?

After my guests left I considered sampling a sausage fly. I resisted the temptation. Somehow the idea of chewing on a large live squirming queen termite with a crunchy anterior and an egg-bloated posterior of creamy and gooey consistency didn't seem all that appealing.

Exposure to new foods often came as either a pleasant or highly unpleasant surprise. One evening I ventured out to the nearby nightclub, dressed in another of my traditional Nigerian outfits made by my local tailor. The sokoto and dashiki, overlying sapara, and fila on my head, were all made of the same attractive dark reddish-brown cloth, with assorted designs in orange, light brown, and yellow colors, including an outline of the African continent.

There were several nightclubs with highlife bands in my Oke-Badan neighborhood. When I first arrived in Nigeria, the rhythmic drumming coming from the clubs caused many sleepless nights, but after months of adjustment the music became mere background noise, and it rarely bothered me as I sat at my desk preparing lesson plans. Most weekends, during school terms, I stayed at home writing tests, grading papers, or preparing lectures and laboratory exercises for the next day's classes. But sometimes I went out alone at night to a local nightclub to drink Star beer, socialize, or dance. I enjoyed listening to the Nigerian music of popular artists like Olatunji, Victor Olaiya, and Cardinal Rex Lawson, and liked dancing the highlife. The dance's graceful rhythmic movements came naturally to me.

That night, as I sat with three Nigerian men I had just met, I spied a pair of eyes, and little else, across the darkened room. I watched as the seemingly disembodied eyes slowly approached. Soon an attractive dark-skinned Nigerian woman was seductively dancing in front of me, holding out her hands for me to join her. We danced, then afterwards sat at a table drinking Star beer. When she said she was hungry, I told her to order what she wanted. Soon a waiter brought a plate to the table. In the dim light, the plate appeared covered with thick slabs of fatty pork. That was my first—and last—exposure to giant African snails, the largest land snails in the world, mollusks with shells roughly the size of softballs, and bodies with a chewy, elastic consistency.

Talking drums and highlife music

Drummers ("onigangan") playing talking drums are a common sight in Nigeria. Talking drums are made from an hourglass shaped piece of wood, and can be of small ("gan gan") or large ("dun dun") size. The drum heads at both ends consist of animal hide or some other membranous material, wrapped around a wooden hoop. Leather cords attached to the hoops run the length of the drum's body.

The drummer, holding the drum tucked under one arm, beats on one head with a carved piece of wood. Squeezing the cords tightens the drum heads, changing the drum's pitch. Because Yoruba is a tonal language, a skilled drummer can replicate the rhythms and intonations of the spoken language, thus making the drums "talk." When used for either entertainment and dancing, or for sending messages, talking drums can be heard from miles away.

Highlife, the music of West Africa from the 1940's to the 1960's, was a fusion of traditional African songs with western style rhythms, such as the rumba and Caribbean calypso. The music derived its name from the fact that bands often played in clubs frequented by the elite, those people living the high life. Highlife bands typically included talking drummers. Highlife music declined in Nigeria during the Biafran War from 1967-70, when bands disbanded and nightclubs closed, but is currently undergoing a minor revival, in spite of the fact that most of the famous highlife musicians are no longer alive or performing.

11

Reluctant Matchmaker

In addition to several of my students, Layiwola, Matthew, Musa, and Olusegun, who often spent time in my home, and one student, Rufus, who lived in one of my spare bedrooms, there were a number of friends and acquaintances, not associated with school, that often visited Adeyoola Chambers. One frequent guest was Abiodun Amusan, a young man who seemed about my own age. I had difficulty judging the age of Nigerians, just as I had with my Vietnamese friends at Southern Illinois. Abiodun worked as a printer's apprentice. He was handsome, with a beaming smile showing off beautiful white teeth against his dark skin. When he visited on Sunday evenings, he was always well groomed and nattily attired in native Yoruba dress. I was helping him with English. Sitting on my couch together, he read to me aloud from some of the books in my paperback library. I enjoyed his company, finding him an interesting and likeable person of good humor, with a polite demeanor and a winning smile.

On several occasions in the evening, we went to a nightclub together, both in native dress. One weekend, he invited me to accompany him on a trip to visit some of his relatives. We traveled by mammy wagon to Abeokuta, a Yoruba city about sixty miles west of Ibadan. Located below famous Olumo rock, Abeokuta is noted for its tie-died fabrics (batiks), and as the birthplace of Nobel Prize-winning Nigerian author Wole Soyinka. On the outward journey, the mammy wagon broke down in an isolated rural area. Rather than wait for another mammy wagon to come along I told Abiodun we would try hitchhiking. I found a large piece of cardboard, wrote "Abeokuta" on it, then stood by the side of the road holding the sign in front of me. The sight of a tall white man holding a cardboard sign alongside a rural road is an uncommon sight in West Africa, and many persons in passing cars and trucks gawked as they drove past.

Soon, a large chauffeur-driven black limousine, sporting small Nigerian flags on both sides of the hood, passed us, then slowed and stopped twenty yards ahead. The dark tinted windows rolled down, and a large man in elegant Nigerian dress motioned for us to enter. Abiodun and I sat on either side of him in the back seat of the spacious air-conditioned car. He registered surprise when I greeted him in Yoruba, then introduced himself as the Western Region's Minister of Finance. He told us he asked his driver to stop because seeing a European hitchhiking was a new experience for him; also, because of my sign, he had assumed I was a mute. We conversed all the way to Abeokuta, where Abiodun and I had a good visit lasting several days. We returned to Ibadan by mammy wagon, and for weeks afterwards, whenever he visited Adeyoola Chambers, Abiodun talked about our hitchhiking adventure, how I was mistaken for a mute, and how special he felt riding in a politician's personal limousine.

A few weeks after our Abeokuta trip, Abiodun visited and asked me to accompany him to a friend's house on a certain evening later in the week. I had a lot of school work to do that week, but he said that it was very important. The friend he wanted me to meet was a young woman, a woman he hoped to marry. He told me that if I accompanied him his female friend would take his courtship more seriously. I assumed he meant that she would be suitably impressed by his having a schoolteacher as a friend, but he may have been referring to other attributes, such as my tall stature, or my whiteness. I was never really sure. Experience had taught me that one's status in West Africa can be considerably elevated by the company one keeps, and that one's friends and companions can exert considerable direct or subtle influences in interpersonal interactions.

Months earlier, I had been an unconscious pawn in such a situation. An acquaintance, Mohammed, a Muslim with four wives, pleaded with me to accompany him to his home village, for reasons that he never fully made clear to me. He was so incessant that I agreed, partly because of our acquaintance, but also because it was an opportunity to travel to another part of Nigeria in the company of someone who knew where they were going. Mohammed and I traveled by lorry to Ondo, a Yoruba town located about eighty miles southeast of Ibadan. He asked me to wear my best clothes, and I was uncomfortably dressed in long black pants, a white dress shirt, and wearing a tie. When we arrived at the Ondo lorry park, we hired a taxi and Mohammed directed the driver to an area in the city.

We entered a building, and Mohammed led me upstairs to a large assembly room. The entire periphery of the room was lined with wooden benches with partitioned seats, about ninety in all. He instructed me to sit in a larger chair located in one corner of the room, then left. The chair was made of a dark wood, perhaps ebony or mahogany. The arms were wide and elaborately carved. After almost an hour of waiting alone in the empty room, dozens of men, all in traditional dress, entered and seated themselves at the other end of the room. The meeting started and the men began talking in Yoruba. Three elderly men, sitting in three larger chairs, ornately carved with high backs, appeared to be moderators. I sensed I was witnessing some kind of hearing, with Mohammed arguing his point, and another man arguing his. Both spoke in Yoruba, gesticulating in animated fashion. On occasion talking turned to shouting. Men periodically rose to their feet, directing comments to either Mohammed or his antagonist. Occasionally, some of the men turned to glance in my direction. I sat on exhibit on my throne-like seat at the opposite end of the room, totally oblivious to what was happening.

After an hour the meeting ended. Mohammed and I returned to Ibadan, arriving late at night. He said nothing to me about the meeting during our return trip, and I never learned what the situation involved, or the outcome. As far as I could surmise, he was involved in some type of dispute in Ondo, involving either property, possessions, or wives—I wasn't sure what—and he believed my presence would somehow sway public opinion in his favor. At the end of the experience, in retrospect, I felt used, uncomfortable playing the role of unwitting stooge.

And so when Abiodun asked me to accompany him to his girlfriend's house, I did so with some reluctance. It didn't seem right, somehow, that Abiodun should rise or fall in favor as a potential suitor based on the fact that he dragged me along as Exhibit A. Still, it was a chance to do a favor for a friend. In spite of my personal feelings, who was I to argue with tradition in such matters? Going with him to his girlfriend's house to help impress her seemed a relatively benign act. I told him, however, that I was not going to verbally plead his case, or try to influence her in any overt way; that it was my opinion that her choice of a suitor was something for her to decide. I told Abiodun I didn't know the girl, and it would be difficult for me to tell her that she should marry him and not other suitors, whoever they were. Abiodun said this was fine, he only wanted me to accompany him as a friend.

On the pre-arranged night Abiodun arrived at Adeyoola Chambers. He was elegantly attired in traditional dress, a dark chocolate brown sapara with a red floral design, and matching trousers. The fila on his head was tipped at the proper rakish angle to indicate that he was eligible. His black sharply pointed leather shoes, looking like lethal weapons, were polished like mirrors. He looked handsome, and when he smiled he showed a mouth full of beautiful straight, white, cavity-free teeth. Truly, a dazzling smile. Were I a Nigerian woman, I would have found him exceptionally attractive and irresistible. We shared a glass of palm wine, toasted to his successful courtship, then went outside and hailed a taxi.

He directed the driver to an area of Ibadan strange to me, and we pulled up near a group of houses. Abiodun requested that I follow him. Within seconds of leaving the taxi, as we walked towards our destination, my presence attracted a group of children, who tagged behind me, and the attention of many interested on-lookers, intently watching from chairs and benches alongside the street, or from windows in nearby houses. I followed Abiodun as he entered a house and walked up stairs to a room on the second floor. There was no door on the room, only a curtain separating it from the main hallway. Off the hallway, there were five other rooms, all behind curtained doorways, and all with a radio or record player with music playing. Abiodun beckoned me to sit down, then left the room. The room was small, simply furnished with a bed, a desk, a bookcase with some books. A schoolbook and notebook lay open on the desk. Apparently the young woman was a student somewhere, and had been studying before we arrived. Her radio was playing highlife music. After ten minutes, Abiodun returned and we sat waiting in the room together.

"I went to find her to inform her that we were here," he said. "She will be here shortly."

"Abiodun, I feel awkward," I said. "I will let you do all the talking."

"No problem, I am happy that you have come," he replied.

After about ten minutes the woman arrived. She was young, in her early twenties. Her hair was intricately plaited in a "pineapple" style. She carried two metal bowls of hot joloff rice with a cooked chicken leg on top, and gave one to each of us. She said a few words in Yoruba to Abiodun, then excused herself. We remained in the room together, I eating the rice, Abiodun just sitting, ignoring his food. I felt uncomfortable, and sensed something was amiss. Abiodun seemed impatient, and as the minutes passed conveyed an impression of being slighted, offended. The woman never returned. After about twenty minutes, my rice eaten, Abiodun stood up and told me it was time to leave.

As we left the house and walked outside to hail a taxi, I saw the girl moving away from a nearby parked car. As Abiodun and I walked past the car the driver stuck his head out the window and greeted me, "Hello, Mr. Sandford." I was completely surprised. How could someone in this strange neighborhood know my name? I looked at the man, and for a moment didn't recognize him. Then suddenly I made the connection. It was Mr. Onibonoje, the English teacher at IBHS. I did not know him well, and was accustomed to seeing him sitting at his desk in the staff room in the mornings before the first class, not behind the wheel of a car at night in an unfamiliar part of Ibadan. Apparently, he had also come to visit the woman, arriving shortly after we did, and was one of her Romeos. It struck me as an amazing coincidence that Abiodun's competition for the woman's favors was one of the few Nigerians I knew by name in a city teeming with millions of potential suitors.

Poor Abiodun. He had some stiff competition. Judging from the woman's behavior, he had come out second best in that evening's round of the dating game. In spite of his strikingly handsome appearance, congenial personality, and friendly winning ways, as a poor printer's apprentice Abiodun was a decidedly inferior suitor compared to Mr. Onibonoje, an older secondary school tutor with his own car.

Abiodun visited me frequently after that. He never spoke again of the young woman, or of his unsuccessful courtship. A few days before I left Nigeria he came to the house with a professional photographer, and we had our pictures taken together on the balcony and on the front porch of Adeyoola Chambers. At our parting he was still working as a printer's apprentice, studying English, hoping to get married, and striving to make something of his life.

12

Vacation Time

Soon it was November 1964. The rainy season had ended, and my first Christmas in Africa was approaching. It hardly seemed like Christmas. The days were hot and dry. In the evening the dust-laden air of the harmattan winds, sweeping down from the Sahara desert, was highlighted by the rays of the setting sun, producing intense red sunsets. A dusty haze shrouded the city. After particularly strong harmattan winds, frequent occurrences during the months of December and January, everything in the house was coated in a layer of fine dust and sand. The greeting cards I received from some of my students, with scenes of Santa Claus in North Pole apparel, or snow-covered trees and quaint English villages, made the holiday mood seem especially incongruous. It was at Christmas that I was most homesick with thoughts of home on Long Island.

Activity was always my solution to melancholy. During my time in Nigeria, I traveled during breaks between school terms, and often on weekends, sometimes hitching a ride on a truck or lorry carrying yams, plantains, or other produce. On most occasions, however, I used the major form of public transport in West Africa, buses or passenger trucks commonly called "mammy wagons," a personification of the adventurous and electric (some would say death-defying) atmosphere associated with travel in much of Africa. I never figured out why they were called mammy wagons, but the term may be derived from the notion of a mother figure—something that is impressively big and holds things.

Mammy wagons were invariably overloaded, overcrowded with people, and an assortment of livestock, goods, foodstuffs and groceries. Baskets and pots filled with produce, sacks of yams, and crates of chickens, usually had first priority, with cramped human passengers sitting or hanging on wherever they could. The drivers behaved as if passenger comfort and safety were non-issues, and the buses often carried a conductor or "agbero," typically a surly young man, who collected the fares. Mammy wagons traveled erratically on no predictable schedule at dangerously reckless speeds on eroded roadbeds and potholed roads, with no posted speed limits or signs to alert motorists of curves, hills, or problematic intersections. Prone to break down, they traveled with no fixed time table. Drivers usually drove like crazed madmen, and showed a complete disregard for passengers by stopping spontaneously and frequently for unscheduled meal stops, conversations with friends spied roadside, or visits to girlfriends in passing villages.

Getting from one location to another was often a time-consuming adventure requiring great patience, as buses stopped frequently along the way to pick up passengers or to load or unload goods. Considering the fact that highway accidents were the major cause of fatality among African PCV's, the slogans emblazoned on front of mammy wagons like "May the Lord be with you," "Be prepared to meet thy maker," or "God help us," seemed ominously appropriate.

The holiday season meant a break between terms at IBHS, and friend Ray and I decided to spend a week or two traveling in Eastern Nigeria. Ray was teaching physics at Government College in Ughelli in the Midwest Region. I took a mammy wagon to Benin, the regional capital, and met Ray. We stayed several days in Benin, famous for its bronzes, then ferried across the Niger River to Enugu, capital of the Eastern Region. On Christmas day we arrived in Port Harcourt, a fast growing port city, and that evening had beer and sandwiches at the bar in the catering rest house, typically frequented by either foreigners in the oil industry or British expatriates. We were the only people there, and spent the entire evening drinking and joking with the Nigerian bartender. Before stumbling out into the night we left silly sayings in the guest book ("Innocent's cucumber sandwiches are an unbelievable taste sensation"), for the benefit of those who followed.

After several days in the Port Harcourt area, we traveled to Oron. From there we took the ferry to Calabar and visited Calabar federal prison, the incarceration location of Obafemi Awolowo, the dissident and highly popular Yoruba leader of the opposition Action Group party of western Nigeria, imprisoned there by political rivals in 1963. Calabar, an attractive city, was founded in 1600 to control slave traffic on the Cross River. We spent New Year's Day in Calabar enjoying the festivities, then hired several men to take us up the Cross River in a dugout canoe. On the trip we passed small simple houses of wood and cane and with thatched roofs, in clear-cuts along the banks, and adults and children navigating up and down the river in canoes. The following day, we visited Ikot Ekpene, famous for its wood carvers, and bought wooden carvings and face masks. There, Ray and I parted and returned to our respective schools for the next school term.

Months sleepily passed. Soon it was April 1965, the beginning of another rainy season. On April 17th some Nigerian PCV's protested in front of the U.S.

embassy in Lagos. New directives from administrative desks in Washington were urging changes for volunteers that were living "too good," and a decision had been made to confiscate some motorcycles. The controversy made little sense to me. Did administrators in Washington have any idea what it was like to try to effectively teach in a tropical country, walking miles to school and arriving in sweat-soaked clothing? To the Nigerian teachers the directives from Washington's bureaucrats seemed ludicrous. They came to school by taxi or in their own cars. They couldn't imagine anyone requiring a Peace Corps volunteer to walk miles to school, then expecting them to have the will and energy to effectively teach. I enjoy hiking, and sometimes during the first year, on nice days, I walked to school. During the second year, political disturbances began to occur and my motorcycle was stolen. I then walked the four mile round trip to school more often, a circumstance my Nigerian co-workers found humorous.

In May of 1965 there was another vacation break between school terms. To fight boredom I volunteered to teach swimming to young boys in a day camp program. Though a swimmer, I had no experience teaching naive Nigerian boys, many with a fear of the water, how to swim. At the beginning of the first lesson I lined them up at the shallow end of the pool and encouraged them to jump en masse into the water, thinking that the cooperative group effort would help overcome any individual fears of the water, and quickly introduce them to the pool. At my command, all thirty boys jumped at once. I was shocked when many plummeted like lead sinkers to the bottom and remained there. I was the only adult at the pool at the time, and the sight of dozens of boys lying on the bottom of the pool set my heart to racing. I jumped into the water and frantically hauled bodies from the bottom, hoisting the "sinkers" up to the pool's edge.

In addition to teaching swimming, I made semi-weekly visits to the Oluyole Cheshire Home, a facility providing care and compassion for physically and mentally handicapped children, either orphaned or rejected by their family. At the home I played games with the children, and read story books to them in English. Many of the children I visited and played with, like little Sunday and four year old Folarunso, had polio, and had to rely on hand-me-down crutches and leg braces inadequate to their needs.

When I wasn't at the pool or the children's home, I took to the road. Wanting to see as much of Nigeria as I could squeeze into my two year stay, I took mammy wagons or hitched rides on lorry's carrying yams or other produce to different cities in the Western Region.

On one school term break I traveled to Badagry, a small coastal town east of the federal capital of Lagos, with friend and former student Segun. Badagry is a place of historical significance. It was an important port during the days of the slave trade, and the site of the first Christian settlement in Nigeria. Across a lagoon, reached by canoe, is Topo island and a lovely rest house retreat. Segun and I stayed at the rest house, the only guests during our three day visit. Relaxing in chairs on the porch, we viewed the lagoon, the ocean beyond, and miles of beautiful white sand beaches with coconut palms. The beautiful scenery and cooling breezes made it a wonderful change from the heat, noise, and crowds, in Ibadan.

I returned to Ibadan and left the following day for Shaki, located one hundred miles northwest of Ibadan. In Shaki, I stayed with Adewale, a recent IBHS graduate, working for the Ministry of Public Health. I shared Adewale's modest accommodations for five days, sleeping on a mat in a small room, with red clay walls and a dirt floor, and without running water or electricity. Shaki was a typical Yoruba town, with houses of a basic and simple architectural design: mud walls, roofs with sheets of zinc metal, small windows for ventilation, a front and back door, and a central middle corridor with rooms on both sides. Often, kitchens and toilets were outdoors in a compound containing kola nut trees, or fruit trees such as citrus, mango, guava, or papaya.

During another term break I traveled to Ijebu-Ode, again with Segun as a companion. We traveled by mammy wagon to the city, located fifty miles south of Ibadan. There we witnessed festivities commemorating the Moslem feast of Id al-Fitr, the official conclusion of the Ramadan fasting period. From a second floor balcony above a main street, Segun and I watched a joyous colorful parade. There were marchers, singers, dancers, and taking drummers. Scattered at intervals in the long parade procession were seven men from Ijebu-Ode, recently returned from their pilgrimage (hajj) to Mecca. Dressed in elegant finery and on horseback, the seven men, now hajjis, were making a triumphant return. The parade was in their honor. After the parade, Segun and I traveled to a small nearby village, where he introduced me to his father, the Oba of Owu. His father's elegant appearance and polite demeanor was in keeping with his position of authority, and he greeted me warmly, welcoming me to his home.

An Oba is a town head chief, a person who traditionally commands much respect among the Yoruba of western Nigeria. The Oba led me into a large room and beckoned me to be seated. After we had taken refreshments, Segun left his chair and moved towards where his father was sitting. He prostrated himself on the floor, honoring his father by addressing him as "kabesi." Segun then began speaking in English, but for a reason I did not understand at the time the Oba interrupted him and told him to converse in Yoruba. Although I could not understand their conversation, I sensed something strange in their relationship.

After their brief conversation, the Oba gave me a tour of his new house, then took me outside and proudly pointed out his new fish ponds, filled with tilapia. Then we walked for about twenty minutes to a nearby village to visit his good friend, the Oba of Ijebu-Ife. During a photo session, I photographed both Obas, and several of their friends and other village dignitaries, standing in front of a hedge of colorful crotons. Late that afternoon Segun and I returned to Ijebu-Ode for the return trip to Ibadan. I bid the Oba goodbye, never realizing that I would meet him again under much less pleasant circumstances.

When I returned to Ibadan, several students helped me celebrate Ramadan in my own way, by slaughtering a goat. My cook/steward at the time, Moses, was proficient at killing and preparing goats. I sent him to a central market area in Ibadan where thousands of goats were available for sale, instructing him to select a healthy ram. When he returned with the ram in tow, he and two of my students, Daniel and Layiwola, slaughtered the animal under the banana trees in my back yard. I watched fascinated as Moses inserted a length of hollow bamboo through a hole in the dead animal's skin. Blowing into the bamboo straw, he inflated the goat, then easily removed the skin from the underlying muscle of the goat balloon. Since I had adopted a largely meatless lifestyle, I kept only a few pieces of meat for myself, and shared the rest with Moses and his extended family, the students, and my neighbors.

As for myself, my own personal Mecca lay not far away in Saudi Arabia, but only several miles from Adeyoola Chambers. On many weekends I grabbed a book, jumped on my Honda, and headed to the Lafia Hotel on Ibadan's outskirts. The Lafia had a pool surrounded by green lawn and lovely lush landscaping. The pool area was un-crowded and open to the general public for three shillings. For only six shillings more I could get a meal of hamburger and chips served poolside. Periodic trips to the Lafia assumed an almost ritualistic quality. I have always been an avid swimmer and love being around water, and relished the chance to spend hours away from crowds and traffic noise in the Lafia's oasis-like surroundings. I sat in a chair poolside, read my book, and indulged myself with a cold quart bottle of Star beer and sausage rolls, punctuated by frequent dips in the nearly empty pool. The garden-like grounds poolside were ablaze with hibiscus and bougainvillea blooms, the air fragrant with the intoxicating scent of frangipani. Relaxing in a cushioned chair by the pool, beneath an umbrella at my own table, the serenity and tranquility of the Lafia seemed like Eden.

In June of 1965, after working in Nigeria for a year, I received a one page typewritten letter in the mail from the White House, signed by President Lyndon Johnson. The letter read as follows:

Dear Mr. Sandford:

I understand that you recently completed you first year of service as a Peace Corps Volunteer.

Today the Peace Corps is recognized throughout the world as a expression of the highest ideals of our nation. That judgment rests on the conduct and accomplishments of you and your fellow volunteers. There can be no more fitting tribute than this to the memory of the man whose vision launched the Peace Corps, our late beloved President John F. Kennedy.

While the role of a single person may be small, it is only through a collective effort such as the Peace Corps that we can hope to build a world in which men and women may share some of the world's bounties and less of its sufferings, and in which nations will offer one another support and respect.

I am proud of your contribution as a Volunteer and confident that your second year of service will continue to reflect credit upon you and the Peace Corps.

Sincerely, Lyndon Johnson

Soon after receiving the letter from President Johnson, my friend Sally, a member of my Nigeria X group, visited Ibadan from Lagos. She worked as a music teacher there. During her visit, we made tentative travel plans for an impending trip to East Africa, then did some Ibadan sightseeing, including a visit to the campus of the University of Ibadan, Nigeria's first university. While we were there, we talked with a man and a young boy selling a large assortment of unique Yoruba thorn carvings, and we each bought some as souvenirs.

August 1965 was approaching, another vacation period between school terms, a time I looked forward to with much anticipation. At long last my travels would take me to the Africa I had dreamed about for so long; the Africa of vast wildebeest herds, a Great Rift Valley, and dramatic sunsets silhouetting graceful long-limbed giraffes moving among scattered acacia trees.

I was one of over one hundred Nigerian Peace Corps volunteers, officials, and friends, on a charter flight to Addis Ababa, Ethiopia, starting point for a long awaited three week visit to East Africa. My excitement was intense. I had done background reading on Ngonongoro Crater National Park in northern Tanzania, and planned to see this awesome natural wonder of landscape and wildlife. I had made no definite plans for the rest of my trip, intending to travel with Sally and several other friends for part of the time, but also to be flexible and to strike off on my own whenever possible, visiting as many other different national parks as time and circumstances allowed.

Biologically-based human differences

A lot of who we are, and what we can or cannot do, is influenced by genes. Contrary to the notion of being master's of our fate, much of our lot in life is predetermined for us at conception by rolls of the genetic dice, something we have absolutely no control over. Genetic differences between individuals, and between groups of people, are real. These differences should not be viewed as deficits, but simply as examples of genetic variations that make us unique. Many scientific studies have documented DNA differences between ethnic groups, including differences in skeletal structure, muscle structure and fiber type, metabolic efficiency, and lung size, just to name a few. If we are aware that such differences exist, we can better understand why many marathons or 10K races are won by East Africans from Kenya or Ethiopia who excel in distance running, and why persons of West African ancestry often excel in sprinting.

The fact that blacks tend to be "sinkers" when it comes to swimming, is partly a consequence of anatomy, denser skeletons, and less body fat. I was not aware of this when I volunteered to teach swimming to young Nigerian boys, and the fact that I am aware of it now does not make me a racist, but helps me better understand why some people are able to do certain things better than other people, and why none of us is perfect.

Anatomical and biological differences between ethnic groups is as real a phenomenon as anatomical and biological differences occurring between individuals. These differences do not make one group more "superior" or "inferior," whether we are considering athletics, politics, or chess playing, but merely help us better understand the world and the human condition. If we set our mind to it, and do the necessary practice, most of us can learn to do many different kinds of things, whether it be juggling, scuba diving, rock climbing, or playing poker. But some of us will always be able to do certain things better than others, because of circumstances over which we have no control; the two sex cells that by chance combined to set our existence in motion. Genetic differences between people are real, but these DNA differences do not, and should not, confer rank.

Yoruba thorn carvings

Thorn carvings are a wonderful example of contemporary Nigerian art, or tourist art, quite different from traditional art. Although the carvings are often displayed in museums with other forms of African folk art, or as interior decorations in the homes of Nigerians as representations of their cultural identity, they are commonly sold to Western tourists visiting Africa. As an art form thorn carving began in the 1950's by a Yoruba artist and wood carver named Justus Akeredolu. As a young man in Owo, he began carving figures from the thorns of wild cotton trees ("ata egun-egun"). His unique art creations gained growing popularity, partly because the sculptures portrayed Yoruba people engaged in their daily activities. His skill at making carvings from forest tree thorns, and the popularity of his miniature creations, led to the establishing of his own sculpture studio, and his growing fame as the father of the new art style of thorn carving.

The woody thorns used for the carvings come in a variety of colors, ranging from pale yellows, to light reds, and rich browns. Thorns also vary in size and shape; some are small and pointy, whereas others can be large (up to twelve cm. long and seven cm. thick). Carvers use darker thorns to carve human faces and limbs, lighter colored thorns to make the torsos. Thorns are individually carved to make heads, bodies, and appendages, then glued together to create human figures. Thorns are also used to carve footstools, effigies, food items, gourds, bowls and cups, tools such as oars or spears, and other objects. Larger objects, such as long boats or entire palm trees, are not carved from thorns, but from larger pieces of wood.

During my time in Nigeria, I purchased ten lovely thorn carvings. These included carvings depicting: a palm wine tapper carrying gourds and climbing apparatus on his back; a kneeling woman with a baby strapped on her back offering a sacrificed chicken at a shrine, consisting of a totem ("ere") in the form of a human mask; a standing drummer playing a talking drum; a seated market woman selling five fish in a large red bowl; a woman carrying a basket filled with sticks of fire wood; and six people traveling in a foot long dugout canoe laden with yams and other produce. The Yoruba people portrayed engaged in the daily activities of village life in the carvings are no larger than several inches tall. The heads of the carvings, regardless of the activity portrayed, are disproportionately smaller than the body, and all show the same emotionless facial expression. The dark colored thorns used to create the heads show faces with similarly carved prominent facial landmarks: tiny slits for the eyes and mouth, bumps for ears, and dots and pinches for the nostrils.

Because of the delicate and fragile nature of the carvings, the figures I purchased did not survive the long voyage home in a shipping crate. When I finally unpacked them most had dislocated heads and broken or missing appendages. While a single Nigerian thorn carving would not be worth much in today's art market, a collection of about a dozen of these carvings, in good condition, was recently estimated as worth from $2,000-3,000 by an Antiques Roadshow appraiser.

The eighteen Nigeria X volunteers for the Western Region with the Premier of the Western Region, Chief Samuel L. Akintola (middle, front) and an education officer (far right) at Government House, Ibadan, June 1964. At far left front row are Peace Corps Director for the Western Region, George Sealey, and Deputy Director Alice O'Grady. I am the tall guy with the fat face in the back row, far left.

IBHS student Musa Momah and I, October 1964. I have already lost twenty pounds since arriving in Nigeria.

The Oke-Badan section of Ibadan and the house, Adeyoola Chambers (middle, center), where I lived for two years.

The view from the balcony of my home, Adeyoola Chambers, on Liberty Stadium Road, Ibadan. Observing streets scenes from my balcony, I often saw children carrying water in basins or buckets on their heads.

Bose, the egg girl, with her guinea fowl eggs, at the steps leading up to the back door of my house, Adeyoola Chambers, in Ibadan, November 1964.

Other women selling eggs often came to Adeyoola Chambers, but I told them I bought all my eggs from Bose. They always accepted my refusal politely, and with good humor.

The school compound and classroom blocks at IBHS. The staff room is at the far right.

Reviewing the parts of the human digestive system with some of the Form IV biology students in the biology classroom at IBHS, with the help of an old wall chart and a rough-surfaced blackboard.

The student officers of Williams House, one of the four boarding houses at IBHS, along with myself (boarding house master), and the assistant house master, March 1965. Seated to my right is student Rufus Obe.

By my bookcase at home. On the lower shelf are the twin ibejis I bought from the old woman at Beatrice's shop, and also eight thorn carvings.

Sunday and Folarunso, two of the children I visited at the Oluyole Cheshire Home in Ibadan.

The Oba of Owu (fourth from left), and his friend the Oba of Ijebu-Ife (fifth from left), and other village dignitaries I met during my first visit to the Oba's house and compound near Ijebu-Ode.

Babatunde, my palm wine tapper.

Mrs. Idowu and her small shop on the side of Liberty Stadium Road, Ibadan. I was her faithful and frequent customer for two years.

My friend Sally, with a man and a boy selling their thorn carvings, on the campus of the University of Ibadan.

Three talking drummers who visited me at Adeyoola Chambers one Sunday. When they began drumming on their "gan gan" below my balcony, I came out into the street to dance and give each a shilling.

13

Animals, Animals.
East Africa Beckons

The Ethiopian Airlines charter taxied down the runway, then lifted off from Lagos International Airport; at long last, my much awaited trip to East Africa had begun. It was late August, 1965. As a biologist, I went to Africa with high hopes of seeing raw nature, trekking through dense forests filled with giant trees, draped with vines and festooned with bromeliads and orchids, alive with the sight and sounds of wild animals. Over a year spent working at IBHS adjacent to congested and noisy Ijebu Bye-Pass in the densely crowded Oke-Ado area of Ibadan, the largest city in black Africa, was not what I imagined my African experience would be like.

In fifteen months, the wildest animals I had seen were cattle emaciated with sleeping sickness, domesticated pygmy goats, head-bobbing agama lizards that perched on the walls around my home and always seemed to be scurrying about engaged in courtship or territorial displays, and the geckos that nightly patrolled my living room walls in search of moths and mosquitoes.

Many interesting insects, and other invertebrates, sometimes infiltrated my home. Insect invasions were especially common after the first rains of the rainy season, a phenomenon that often triggered social insects like winged termites ("sausage flies") to disperse from their nests en masse, like rising clouds of smoke, on their flight to establish new colonies elsewhere. Of these uninvited house guests, the most dramatic and unusual invasion occurred late one evening, weeks before my scheduled departure to East Africa.

Lying in bed naked, sweating profusely, and trying to fall asleep one uncomfortably hot and humid night during the rainy season, I heard a faint crackling sound. The strange sound reminded me of a distant forest fire, or a hand crumpling dry paper, and seemed to be coming from the living room, just beyond my closed bedroom door. I lay awake listening to the sounds, trying to identify their source. Finally, confused and curiosity aroused, I lifted up the mosquito netting, left my bed, and opened the bedroom door.

The sounds were louder now. I stood in the doorway peering into the living room, my eyes slowly adjusting to the darkness. Moonlight was coming through the living room windows. The faint crackling sounds were louder, but I still couldn't locate the source of the diffuse sound. Then, sensing subtle movements, my eyes shifted downwards to a snakelike apparition, and I saw what appeared to be a long length of curved ribbon, about four inches wide, on the floor.

Whoa ... what the? ... the ribbon was moving! I rubbed my eyes, peering more closely at the dark moving band extending the entire length of the room. It was too long, too large, to be a snake. Are those raisins? My mind was racing. Is that a flowing stream of raisins moving across my living room floor? I looked more critically at the dark ribbon near my bare feet. It was coming from the direction of my kitchen, traversing the floor only several feet away from my bedroom door.

The dimness of the moonlit room and the crackling sinuous black ribbon undulating across the red poured concrete floor seemed unreal. Was I awake, or only hallucinating? Can raisins move? It took several minutes for my brain to finally register reality. The individual entities in the moving ribbon were not raisins at all—but ants! Driver ants. A huge colony of driver ants, moving in a tightly configured winding column, with only a few scattered outlier ants, probably scouts, to break the integrity of the mass of closely packed ant bodies. In width, the column was at least a dozen ant bodies wide, and several ants deep, with ants moving atop other ants. I pulled a chair into the doorway and sat watching the spectacle of an unbroken moving insect column for the next hour. I sat, in a gathering pool of sweat running off my body, until the first light of dawn. There had to have been hundreds of thousands of ants in the colony. They entered the house through the back door, moved through the kitchen, then into the living room, finally exiting under the balcony door and over the balcony to Liberty Road below.

When the last stragglers making up the rear guard departed, I went to my kitchen only to find it as Mother Hubbard had—completely bare. Every food item, unprotected by encasement in metal or glass within pincer-reach, was gone. The ants had eaten through the paper wrapping covering the bread, leaving only a few scattered crumbs. They had consumed the entire large hidden cache of sausage rolls that I enjoyed eating with my evening bottle of Star beer. Only a tin of tea bags, and cans of stew and tomato sauce for joloff rice, remained unconsumed and unmolested.

In addition to insects, there was the matter of snakes. In spite of the lectures during the training program warning us about the dangerous snakes of West Africa, and although I was ever on the lookout for them, I only encountered two snakes during my entire two years in Africa. The first occasion occurred only several weeks after I arrived at IBHS, when a snake in two pieces was presented to me by the school bursar in a shoe box in the staff room. One of the 2nd form boys had committed some infraction, and as punishment had been cutting grass with a machete near a clump of trees on the school compound. When the harmless Emerald snake (*Gastropyxis smaragdina*) moved within machete distance, the boy automatically hacked it in half. Sensitivity to the plight of animals, the notion of protecting animals and wildlife preservation generally, especially concerning snakes, was a foreign idea to my students. To them, all snakes were dangerous and deserving of death. I accepted the snake for the biology program as graciously as I could, but informed everyone within earshot that in future I preferred whole live snakes rather than dead snakes in halves.

My second snake encounter occurred when a Nigerian man unexpectedly showed up at IBHS one morning. He was dressed in Western-style clothing, and spoke good English. He told Mr. Adebunmi, the school secretary, that he wanted to see the science teacher. After we were introduced, he said he wanted to donate an egg-eating snake to the science department so that the students could observe its feeding habits. This was exciting news. I had done background reading on the snakes of West Africa during the training program, and knew a few facts about egg-eating snakes and their fascinating habits. Assuming I would never be lucky enough to observe a live egg-eating snake, I couldn't believe my good fortune that one had suddenly presented itself in such fashion.

The school library had no books about egg-eating snakes, but fortunately I had a personal copy of *West African Snakes* by G. Cansdale, one of the few books I had brought with me from the States. During the last week of the training program at Columbia, I spent an afternoon visiting different book stores in Manhattan, finally locating a copy for purchase.

The book gave a brief description of the snake, including a color drawing. It described the snake's unique feeding habits, and harmless nature. According to author Cansdale egg-eating snakes are nocturnal and arboreal, often found near weaver-bird nests. The color drawing in the book showed a brown snake with darker patterns of banding and spotting. The inactive snake the man pulled out of the cloth bag he carried was much darker and of a nearly uniform black coloration, but in consulting Cansdale's description he mentioned that egg-eating snakes can occur with many color variations, including specimens in varying shades of brown and black. Assuming I had a black color variant of the egg-eating snake, *Dasypeltis scabra*, I thanked the man for his generosity, and prepared an enclosure for the snake in a cracked aquarium in the biology classroom.

For the next several weeks each morning, soon after arriving at school, I removed the wooden lid and placed fresh guinea fowl eggs in the aquarium, but the snake was lethargic and showed no interest in eating. Assuming that such snakes in nature find and eat only fresh eggs, I diligently removed uneaten eggs, and replaced them with fresh eggs, on a daily basis. But the snake ignored the eggs, becoming increasingly inactive. It remained curled up in a corner of the aquarium, barely moving.

One morning, I lifted the enclosure top to remove the uneaten egg from the previous day, and to add a fresh one bought from home. I picked up the listless snake to inspect it for possible wounds or injuries, and discovered that it was dead. At the end of the school day I put the rigid coiled corpse in a small box, got on my Honda, drove several miles to the University of Ibadan, and searched out the science building. When I got there a receptionist directed me to a biology laboratory, where I informed a Nigerian instructor that I had an egg-eating snake to donate to the university. He said he was knowledgeable about Nigerian snakes, and that the snake would be a useful addition to their zoology collection.

When I removed the snake from the box the man did a double-take, quickly moving backwards. It was only then, after his brief examination and confirmation of identity, that I learned that the snake I had plied with eggs was not an egg-eating snake at all, but a spitting or black-necked cobra (*Naja nigricollis*). I had been reaching into a lidded aquarium almost daily for several weeks, trying to feed guinea fowl eggs to a highly venomous spitting cobra!

Afterwards, I conjectured about the well dressed stranger who had visited IBHS to donate the snake. Had he, like myself, been confused regarding its true identity? Or was it an ingenious subterfuge by an unfriendly Nigerian to do in a CIA mole; to rub out one more unwanted agent of Neo-colonialism disguised as a Peace Corps volunteer? I was never sure. In recalling the situation I feel fortunate that the lesson of the importance of self-verification and of questioning the knowledge and authority of others, especially on potentially serious matters, was not more painfully learned.

But West Africa, IBHS, and altered Nigerian natural habitats, devoid of wildlife because of over-hunting or exploding human population growth, was all behind me now. Soon I would be on a chartered flight to East Africa, and its savannahs with vast herds of zebra and wildebeest. I could hardly wait.

Egg-eating snakes and Spitting cobras

Egg-eating snakes are found in many parts of Africa. There are several different species. All are harmless, adapted to live exclusively on a diet of fresh bird eggs. They have no teeth, and their mouths can open to an astonishing degree, enabling them to swallow eggs several times their own diameter. As an egg travels down the snake's gullet it encounters unique short bony projections extending from the snake's backbone. These projections crack the egg. The snake swallows the egg's contents, spitting out the crushed shell.

Spitting cobras are another of natures serpent wonders. Unlike other cobras, the openings of its poison fangs are not at the tip, but instead face forward. When disturbed, and as a defensive reaction, spitting cobras "spit" a spray of venom that can travel up to several feet. Any venom touching the eyes of its victim causes intense pain and inflammation. The "spitting" is solely a defense against intruders; to kill its prey the snake uses its fangs like other cobras. Spitting cobras are usually a dark slate gray color, but brown color variants are known. In all likelihood, the cobra I mistook for an egg-eating snake was either old or sick when I received it. This might explain why it was always inactive and never exhibited any aggressive behavior or reared up in a threat display, extending the specialized elongated ribs in its neck region, spreading its distinctive cobra "hood."

14

Addis Ababa

Departing Lagos, and after a brief stop in Ft. Lamy, Chad, our plane continued east. Somewhere over Central Africa, now the Democratic Republic of Congo, we encountered a frightening storm. The Ethiopian stewardesses had just served a meal of tomatoes stuffed with runny fillings, and other creamy concoctions, that did not lie well in the stomachs of passengers on a bumpy ride. The frightened look on the face of one young stewardess did little to calm the fears of an infrequent flier like myself. During the rough trip, amidst a terrifying lightning storm, nearly everyone lost food that flew or fell off their trays, and several passengers lost what little lunch they had already eaten.

We arrived in Addis Ababa, Ethiopia's capital, and scattered our separate ways. Everyone had made different individual or group plans for the trip. The only instructions, set by charter organizers, was that everyone rendezvous at the airport in Kampala, Uganda for the return flight to Lagos in three weeks. Several volunteers and I decided to explore Ethiopia before heading elsewhere, and that first evening in Addis we decided to have an authentic Ethiopian meal. When we inquired about the location of a neighborhood restaurant frequented by locals, un-catered by Westerners, we received rather complicated instructions from a shopkeeper, and spent nearly an hour aimlessly walking down side streets and back alleys.

"Didn't the man say that the restaurant was further up the street that we just turned off of," said one of the women in our group of six.

"No," said John, a volunteer from Nigeria IX, who had assumed the role of leader. "He said up this street and to the left. It should be easy to find. He said there was a canopy over the front door."

After further walking and unsuccessful searching, we had nearly given up our quest for traditional Ethiopian cuisine as a lost cause, when we came upon a place that appeared to be the long-sought restaurant. It had an arbor in front, and a brick paved flower-lined path leading to a modest exterior. Above the front door, there was a striped awning and what appeared to be a sign, a length of red wood with Amharic lettering. On either side of the door were two small shrubs in large ornate red pots.

Upon knocking, we were greeted by a simply attired middle-aged woman. When we told her that her restaurant came highly recommended, she smiled weakly, hesitated momentarily, then led us into a large room, motioning us to sit at a round table. We told her we needed no menus, and requested the house special for six.

During the long wait that followed, all of us commented on the restaurant's homey lived-in atmosphere. It had to be authentic given its off-the-beaten track location and rustic appearance, and the fact that it obviously catered to a local clientele. In the room there was just the single large wicker table at which we were sitting, and six unmatched chairs, two of which the woman and a young girl had retrieved from an adjoining room. Perhaps, we thought, other patrons were dining in other rooms out of view. Over an hour passed. During our wait we heard loud talking and occasional yelling from the kitchen, accompanied by the sounds of doors opening and closing, pots and pans clanging. Occasionally the faces of small children appeared briefly in the doorways of adjacent rooms, shyly peeking from behind curtains.

Eventually the woman appeared with a large serving dish holding what looked like a gigantic thin gray pancake several feet across. Around the edge of the pancake, neatly arranged at intervals like the numbers on a clock face, were a dozen small piles of assorted curried meats, grated cheeses, nuts, apricots, figs and other fruits, and what appeared to be dollops of yoghurt or cottage cheese. We dug in, ripping off chunks of the pancake to gather up and transfer the contents of the tasty piles around its periphery to our waiting mouths. It was delicious food, ample and filling; both pancake and toppings were quickly demolished. As we were eating, many different people, apparently members of the household or alerted neighbors, came into the room at various times to observe us as we devoured the food like a pack of starving wolves. About midway through the meal, we realized the reality of our situation.

We weren't in a restaurant at all, but a private residence. We had invaded some family's home! Instead of becoming angry or calling the police, the woman and her relatives, apparently overwhelmed and honored by our surprise visit, had quickly mobilized and prepared us a delicious and memorable home-cooked meal.

The large flat thin crepe-like pancake we ate with relish is called injera, Ethiopian flat bread, a traditional food in Ethiopia. For drink, the family gave us tej,

Ethiopian honey wine, a traditional beverage made from fermented honey and a special kind of hops. Tej is similar to mead, the world's oldest fermented drink. Ethiopians believe that when King Solomon first met the Queen of Sheba, they toasted one another with tej. The woman was so accommodating and appreciative of our visit that we offered her generous payment for her wonderful meal. She refused to accept the money at first. Reluctantly, after much insistence, she did, accompanied by bowing, smiling, and other expressions of gratitude and good will.

We spent the next day sight-seeing: Jubilee Palace, Africa Hall, the lions in Haile Selassie's private collection, and Trinity Church. As we explored the church, I became separated from my companions. Alone in a room, I walked through a partially opened doorway, entering another large circular room empty of people. There were dark red long curtains hanging on the walls. As I walked and gawked, looking upwards at the ceiling, stained glass windows, and historical artifacts, I inadvertently entered an inconspicuously roped off area, only realizing I had done so when I noticed an armed guard rapidly approaching. He confronted me, speaking in good English.

"Excuse me sir. You cannot be here, this is a private area."

"Oh, I'm sorry," I said. "The church you mean?"

"No sir, this area where you are," he replied, pointing out a red velvet rope barrier I'd breached.

"Oh, I'm very sorry," I said, noticing for the first time the low barrier less than two feet off the floor.

"You must leave now, sir. You are standing on the sacred seal, and his highness is waiting to enter. He wishes to go to his private chapel."

Looking down at the floor, I saw that I was indeed standing on some kind of emblem, then, looking up, I saw other uniformed guards standing at attention by a nearby curtain. As I was ushered out of the area by the guard, I turned before going through the doorway, just in time to see him enter the room. I only caught a brief glimpse of him as he entered from behind a curtain, but recognized him immediately from pictures I had seen—his "Imperial Majesty Haile Selassie I, Conquering Lion of the Tribe of Judah, King of Kings and Elect of God." He had been awaiting my departure from behind the curtain, on his way to private prayers.

Haile Selassie

Haile Selassie, born Tafari Makonnen, was a man whose life was closely linked to the modern history of the country of Ethiopia, once called Abyssinia. Born in 1891, he reigned as Emperor of Ethiopia from 1930 until his death in 1974. When Ethiopia was invaded by Italy in 1936 he fled to England. He returned in 1941 with Allied troops and was restored to the throne. He was an advocate for civil disobedience, when warranted, to remedy circumstances of social injustice or to restore freedom to the oppressed. He was one of the few world leaders of modern times who, like Dwight Eisenhower, a man he counted among his friends, actually led troops in combat. A popular head of state, and one of the most decorated men in the world, he is often remembered for his distinguished presence at the funeral of President John F. Kennedy. He is known as the religious symbol for God incarnate among the followers of the Rastafarian movement.

15

Visit to the Hyena Man

After another day sightseeing in Addis Ababa with my companions, I decided to strike off on my own for eastern Ethiopia. I took a train from Addis to Dire Dawa. From there I traveled by bus to the ancient walled city of Harar, a city with over eighty mosques, three dating from the tenth century. Arriving at the train station, I was immediately surrounded by children, vendors, and beggars. One vendor, a man selling assorted jewelry and leather goods, desperately pleaded with me to buy the skin of a Colubus monkey which he was carrying. He was so insistent that I eventually relented and bought the beautiful black and white pelt, a decision I have regretted ever since.

From the station I took a "taxi"—a horse draw cart—to the home of some Peace Corps volunteers, who put me up for two days. I chose Harar over other potential destinations because I remembered reading, about ten years earlier, when in high school, a National Geographic article about Ethiopia. The story featured an elderly man in Harar who communicated with wild hyenas. The article and accompanying photographs had impressed me.

Now that I had made it to Harar, I wanted to find the "hyena man," even though it seemed unlikely that he would still be alive. The National Geographic photo showed an old wizened man, short and slight, with a highly wrinkled face.

I spent several hours sightseeing, sauntering through both the Christian and Moslem markets. I watched women at a weaver's cooperative making beautiful multi-colored baskets. During lunch at the Ras Hotel, I tried my first artichokes. Afterwards, I rested for several hours on an outdoor patio, enjoying the scenery, in anticipation of my visit to the hyena man later that evening. I had inquired about him earlier from a shopkeeper.

"Excuse me, do you know of the man who talks to the hyenas?"

"Yes," he replied. So the hyena man was still alive. I was surprised, it hardly seemed possible.

"Please, how can I find him?"

The man replied quickly, as if he had been asked the question often.

"Along the wall. Go late in the evening, and you will find him by the wall."

"Which wall?" I asked. "There is a lot of wall around the city."

"Just walk along the wall after dark," he replied. "You will find him."

The shopkeeper's response impressed me with a curious mixture of both pleasant surprise and disquieting ambiguity. Harar was large, with a considerable expanse of wall surrounding the perimeter of the old city, but knowing that the hyena man was still alive created for me more excitement than consternation. After dark that evening, accompanied by a female PCV who lived and worked in Harar, I began searching for the hyena man. We walked around nearly the entire outer walls of the old city before we eventually found him. He was sitting on a rock, wearing only a pair of old cotton shorts, beside a small campfire. The fire, encircled by a ring of large rocks, was in a clearing about twenty-five yards from the wall. After explaining in pidgin English that we knew of him and were interested in meeting, he motioned for us to sit on one of the rocks located several feet from the fire. We each took a rock, then watched as the old man reached into a small worn leather bag hanging around his neck and pulled out several pieces of what we eventually identified as green and moldy, highly odoriferous, strips of meat.

He started chanting. He chanted, occasionally calling out, for several minutes. When I finally diverted my rapt attention away from the old man, I became aware of dozens of pairs of light-reflecting eyes, visible in the darkness several hundred yards from the fire. At first glance, in the gloom, they looked to be large dogs.

The old man continued slowly swaying and chanting. The eyes moved closer. Then I heard the yips, and bizarre laughing vocalizations, typical of hyenas. Before I had any further time to react to the situation, our little campfire was literally surrounded by nearly a dozen adult spotted hyenas. Some were brazen and fearless, and came within a few feet of the fire. The old man had given us no idea what might happen or how to react, but both my companion and I sat frozen on our stone seats, barely moving. From unnerving experiences with wild animals in the past, including a scary physical encounter with a black bear in Wyoming, and with a roaming dog pack in Illinois, one of which left tooth marks in my thigh, I knew that the best strategy to adopt in a close encounter with any large and potentially dangerous animal is to avoid eye contact, and to make no sudden movements or attempts to run. After the hyenas quickly approached and surrounded us, I sat unmoving with my head facing the hyena man, only glancing at the animals from the corners of my eyes.

To my right side, and only several feet away, were several large hyenas, their eyes about level to my own. They had massive muscular forequarters, sloping shoulders, huge jaws and salivating mouths, large canine teeth, and a powerfully fetid "could-have-knocked-me-over" breath. The hyena man held up the aged meat pieces and the hyenas took them, surprisingly gently, from his hands. We remained watching, silent and spell bound, a mixture of apprehension and amazement, as he continued to pull meat strips from his pouch. Several times he put a meat bit in his mouth for one especially bold animal to take.

He continued pulling strips of meat from his bag, feeding them to those animals daring enough to approach the fire. At one point he held out a moldy meat scrap at arms length in my direction, and a huge hyena head, with torn ears and a scarred face, moved forward to within a foot of my face. Saliva was drooling from its lips. I could feel my heart pounding against my rib cage. Perhaps visiting the hyena man in this isolated location late at night, far removed from any hospital or first aid station, hadn't been such a good idea after all.

He continued feeding the animals for several minutes more until his pouch was empty. Then, as if on cue, the hyenas quickly departed, apparently well rehearsed in a familiar routine. Before I realized the show was over they were gone, except for luminous eyes, dark shapes, and their eerie cackling and yipping coming from the blackness around our nearly dead campfire. Once they had gone, I looked more closely at the old man, especially noting the fact that he had all ten of his fingers. We tipped him for his amazing performance, leaving him sitting alone by his small fire. I left feeling fortunate that I had found him, and in a state of great excitement, my heart still racing, happy to be departing with all of my anatomy intact.

Hyena Man of Harar

Harar is considered the fourth holiest city of Islam. In the sixteenth century, a wall four meters high, and containing five gates, was built that completely encircled the city. Today, Harar remains one of the oldest walled cities in Africa with its walls still intact.

The hyena man I met in 1965 was, as much as I can tell, the original and first official Harar "hyena man." He began feeding meat to wild hyenas sometime in the 50's, although there are stories of Harar people feeding hyenas during a famine in the late nineteenth century, as an appeasement gesture to discourage hyenas from carrying off small children, or attacking livestock during times of drought. I am not certain when the old man died, but there is now a tradition in Harar of feeding hyenas on a nightly basis for the benefit of tourists visiting the city. In 2002, according to a news report, there were only two hyena men in Harar. Concerned that the tradition was dying out, several young boys were being trained to carry on the unusual practice.

16

Ngorongoro Crater

The next day I left Harar, returned to Addis Ababa by train, then boarded a bus to Nairobi, Kenya. After a day in Nairobi, several PCV's and I bussed south to Arusha in northern Tanzania, and from there traveled in a rented Volkswagen to Lake Manyara National Park. At park headquarters, we were joined by a park guide who escorted us around the park. We saw cape buffalo, giraffe, hippo, large flocks of pelicans and flamingos, and drove dangerously close to a large bull elephant that suddenly appeared from behind some shrubbery. The guide then directed us to some sleeping lions, informing us that Manyara lions had the unusual behavior of resting in the lower branches of trees. I ran through several rolls of 36-exposure slide film in Manyara, including a dozen photos of two lionesses snoozing on the lower branches of a tree.

From Lake Manyara we drove the short distance to Ngorongoro Crater, which adjoins the very large Serengeti National Park at its southeast corner. This was the destination of my dreams. Ngorongoro is the world's largest extinct volcanic crater, fifty miles in circumference on the inside, and approximately fifteen miles in diameter. The crater rises some 10,000 feet above the surrounding countryside. There are a wide variety of habitats within the confines of the caldera, including a large salt lake in its center, dry grassland, tall grass, thorn bush, bamboo thickets, and rain woods on the crater slopes. At the hotel on the crater rim we hired a land rover. As we slowly descended into the crater along a winding dirt road, I was enthralled by the scene below me. The crater floor was dotted everywhere with what at first appeared to be scattered rocks. As we further descended, and the dark masses came into focus, each dark "rock" on the grassland carpet of the crater floor morphed into an animal. Animals were everywhere.

We spent the entire day in the crater, lunching under acacia trees on a hillside overlooking the lake, with herds of zebra and wildebeest visible in every direction. I snapped dozens more photographs, this time of grazing zebra. Driving along the shore of the large lake on the crater floor, we stopped for fifteen minutes to watch a large pack of African wild dogs drinking, lying about, and playing.

The day was clear with a slight cooling breeze. Clouds passing over the crater's rim resembled waves meeting a reef crest, or breaking on a rocky shore. Though I had no telephoto lens for my camera, as we toured the crater, I took close-up pictures of plains zebra, wildebeest, bushbuck, lions, black rhino, and the wild dogs. At one point our land rover, and two others that had joined us in a joint cooperative effort to look for lions in some tall grass, came too close to a small group of black rhinos. As our land rover was moving away from the others, I heard shouting and looked back. A rhino was charging one of the other land rovers, and an Indian women in a billowing blue sari was screaming in response.

Leaving Ngorongoro, we returned to Arusha, then traveled on to Moshi, stopping briefly at a picturesque mosque. Before returning to Nairobi we stopped at Mt. Kilimanjaro, where I hiked for several hours up the trail at the mountain's base. On the trail I met a young Kikuyu boy. He walked with me for over an hour, pointing out interesting plants and landscape features along the trail.

Upon returning to Nairobi I decided to strike off on my own, planning to rendezvous with friends in Mombasa several days later. I said goodbye to my travel companions. The next day, before leaving, I toured Nairobi Game Park just outside the city. I saw a wide variety of wildlife, including a photogenic majestic dark-maned lion. That evening, while having a drink in the bar at the New Stanley Hotel, I struck up conversation with an Englishman. When I told him I was planning to take the morning bus to Mombasa, he cautioned me not to sit in the back. When I asked why, he replied "because that's where the bloody Masai sit."

Ngorongoro Crater, then and now

Approximately 40,000 large animals lived in the crater in the 1960's, the greatest concentration of large wild animals on the face of the earth! More than thirty different mammal species were present, predominantly large herds of zebra and wildebeest.

Today, Ngorongoro crater, and the contiguous Ngorongoro Conservation Area, remains one of the world's most amazing natural spectacles, although much changed from the crater I visited in 1965. There still are impressive populations of large animals living within the crater, but numbers have dropped to about 25,000 animals. The crater is home to a large

African lion population, but there have been drastic declines in numbers of black rhino, and significant declines in wildebeest and certain antelope species. Sadly, the wild dogs have completely disappeared.

Over 40,000 Masai tend their herds of cattle, sheep, and goats in the conservation area, and grazing is allowed on the crater floor. There are now more hotels, and accommodations for tourists willing and able to pay the high prices are much plusher than they were in the 60's.

Ngorongoro Crater Lodge on the crater's rim boasts an opulent stylish interior with crystal chandeliers, large gilt mirrors, carved Zanzibar wood paneling embellished with gold leaf, and voluptuous raw silk curtains. You can stay in a sumptuous suite, tended by your own personal butler. He is available to serve you tea in bed, or scatter rose petals on the surface of your bath water.

17

Mombasa Bound

The next day, I went to the bus park early and boarded the Mombasa bus. Recalling the Englishman's advice about not sitting in the rear, risking exposure to Masai passengers, I got on and immediately moved to the last seat in the back. Expecting that my travel experience would be similar to previous trips using public transport in Africa, I anticipated many travelers, and having to share a cramped space with women market vendors carrying infants on their backs, and with goats, chickens, or assorted produce. To my surprise the bus was nearly empty, except for a few passengers who sat up front near the driver. The bus was old, rusted, and covered with dirt. Most of the windows were closed, coated with grime and red dust.

In hurrying to the bus park from my hotel to catch the first bus, I hadn't eaten breakfast. Hungry, and uncertain how long the trip might last, I purchased food from a local vendor at the bus station. Buying from unknown vendors in the tropics is always risky business, but hunger pangs made me relax my defenses. In Nigeria a common food item sold by street vendors are round dough balls made of flour, water and sugar, deep fried in peanut or palm oil. These pastries, roughly similar to oily donut holes, are sold by women and young girls from glass cases carried expertly balanced on their heads. In Nigeria these dough ball concoctions are called puff-puffs, and I was pleasantly surprised to see a young Kenyan girl standing by the door of the bus selling puff-puff look-alikes. In Kenya they are called mandazi.

I purchased six from the girl and ate the first one immediately. It tasted differently from Nigerian puff-puffs; more doughy in texture, extremely oily (the newspaper the girl wrapped the others in quickly became grease covered), and less tasty, but I was hungry and wolfed down the remaining five once I took my back seat in the bus.

As I was finishing the last of the mandazi, the bus left for the 307 mile trip to Mombasa. It was a hot and dusty day, and the back of the bus quickly became oppressively warm. Every window I tried to open was stuck shut, and after several hours on dusty bumpy roads I began to feel ill. My head ached, my stomach was queasy. The bus made relatively few scheduled stops, but occasionally picked up or let off passengers roadside. At one unscheduled stop near noon, almost halfway into the trip, in a desolate barren area that fit the description of the proverbial middle-of-nowhere, six young Masai warriors standing roadside hailed down the bus. They boarded, and moved straight to the back. I was quickly surrounded. They were all carrying spears. Apparently they had recently engaged in some type of strenuous activity, for all were sweating liberally.

The men wore almost no clothing, naked except for a long cloth strip loosely worn serape-like over their shoulders. All were of slender build, and taller than me. At 6'3" tall, I was accustomed to standing out in a group, not being dwarfed by it. The men had jewelry hanging from their pierced and stretched earlobes, and their hair was held rigidly in place by a mixture of cow dung and red mud. Standing roadside they presented an elegant stylish appearance. Boarding the bus, they moved in an elegant, dramatically fluid manner. But now, sitting surrounded by them up close and personal, it was my olfactory, not my visual sense, that prevailed. I quickly realized that one's appreciation of beautifully sculptured and elegantly landscaped mud-dung hairdos is inversely proportional to one's proximity to same.

The next hour was uncomfortable, almost unbearable, and seemed to stretch forever like the flat arid landscape of red dirt and scattered scrub through which we drove. I refused to contradict my convictions, and possibly offend the young men, by moving to another seat in the nearly empty bus, but I became more and more wretched as time passed. The back of the bus was stifling hot, the air oppressively heavy with a curious cornucopia of odors. The combining effects of heat, the pungent admixture of dung and sweat, lack of fresh air, the long bumpy ride, and a sole recent meal of greasy mandazi dough balls, together produced a disquieting synergism. I attempted to keep my mind off my upset stomach by conversing with the men in pidgin English, and before they left the bus just before our one and only formally scheduled rest stop at Voi, I purchased one of their spears. It was metal and could be disassembled into 3 separate pieces for easy carrying. The end of the nearly two foot long spear point section was sticky with blood.

Voi lies on the main road between Nairobi and Mombasa, located in a flat desolate area surrounded by arid openness. When we stopped, I left the bus with a terrible headache, a rebelling GI tract, and a burning thirst. At the nearby Voi

Central Hotel, standing outside in the bright sun among a large crowd of Kenyans, I drank a cold orange Fanta which seemed to help—just momentarily.

After walking back to the bus, my sandals kicking up clouds of dry red dust as I moved, the trip resumed and my discomfort returned. I tried closing my eyes and resting, not thinking about how miserable I felt as the bumpy ride progressed. When we finally arrived in Mombasa, about two hours later, it was late afternoon. At the bus station I asked the first person I saw the location of the nearest hotel and quickly began speedwalking, hoping the fresh air and exercise might do me good.

The hotel, whose name I have since forgotten, had an attractive white-washed exterior and a shrub-lined walkway. Inside, there was a beautiful, clean, spacious lobby with a black and white tiled floor. Adjacent to the registration desk was a lounge and indoor patio area with white wicker tables and chairs, a small pool with gurgling fountain, and large potted palm trees. Two large green and white striped awnings, hanging from the second floor balcony above, extended out over the patio area, adding to its outdoorsy ambiance. Several of the tables were occupied by well dressed Caucasian tourists or hotel residents, having what appeared to be late afternoon tea. As I endured waiting for someone ahead of me to register, and then completed the details of my own check-in from a Kenyan desk clerk working in slow-motion, I felt pale and clammy. I started to perspire heavily, and my discomfort intensified. Waves of nausea began to sweep over me. My stomach had finally reached rebellion stage, and I knew that I was going to be sick. But I'd made it this far. Surely I could hold out until I reached my room, I thought.

The clerk handed me a key for a room on the second floor. A young Kenyan bellhop took my bag, and we started up the winding staircase that skirted the patio dining area. As I ascended the stairs I knew that the moment had come, and it suddenly did just as I reached the top landing. With no potted plants or trash receptacles visible, and with little time to react or contemplate alternatives, I doubled over the balcony and vomited a foul torrent of fermenting orange Fanta and semi-digested mandazi dough balls onto one of the striped awnings. The memory trace of the episode is firmly stored away in some nerve cell complex in my cerebrum—a frozen tableau of several proper English ladies looking up from their tea, with looks of horror and amazed disbelief on their faces, at the sounds of retching and the waterfall of vomitus from above.

I spent the rest of the day sleeping in my hotel room, too ill and ashamed to venture forth, until noon the next day. The hotel management was either very kind and understanding or totally astounded by the nature of my grand entrance into their hotel, for no one disturbed me or made any mention of the incident.

The next afternoon I went sightseeing, visiting first the old Moslem quarter, and then Fort Jesus overlooking Mombasa harbor. Mombasa impressed me as a beautiful and uniquely different city. I remember thinking that I had never seen water looking as turquoise blue as the Indian Ocean viewed from the parapets of Fort Jesus.

In the late afternoon I went for a quick swim at Mombasa beach. The beach was nearly deserted except for several groups of children. I was the only person in the water. The day was windy with lots of whitecaps. There were no lifeguards on duty. Because of the rough surf and my unfamiliarity with the beach, I took a quick swim, then left the water. As I removed my wet bathing trunks and showered in the men's changing room minutes later, the only other occupant approached and began talking. Ruggedly handsome, and dressed in proper big game hunter garb, he began conversing as I stood there naked and dripping.

"Hello there, have a good swim," he said with a thick English accent.

"Yes, very invigorating, but the currents a bit strong," I replied.

"It's wise to be cautious, there have been drownings here." he continued. "Peter's my name," he said, and after several more words of introductory banter, "I'm leaving soon in my land rover for a trip into the back country to scout out some new areas. Care to come along?"

He didn't tell me why he was scouting out new areas, but from his outfit and healthy tanned appearance I assumed he worked as some kind of guide for tourists or hunting parties.

"Sounds interesting," I said, "how long will you be gone."

"Not sure," he answered, "a few days, no more than a week. I've got the tents, food, and necessary camping supplies. You could help with gas if you wanted."

His offer was tempting, and one that I might have jumped at under other circumstances, but a week seemed too long a time, and I had already made other plans. He seemed a nice chap, and I apologized for not being able to accept his invitation. In all likelihood he was only being friendly and looking for some companionship, admittedly very atypical behavior for an Englishman, but somehow the idea of spending a week alone in the bush with a burly stranger did not seem prudent, especially considering the circumstances of our meeting. Now, many years later in retrospect, I could shoot myself for turning down his invitation; another adventurous road untaken.

Later that evening, I met up with friend Sally, who I had last seen in Addis Ababa. We had each visited the other in our respective teaching locations back in Nigeria, and I knew her to be a good traveling companion; a friendly and outgoing extrovert, presumptuous enough to insinuate herself into unique situations. Her brash and friendly personality enabled her to engage strangers in a manner that was more childlike and innocent than rude, and that an introvert like myself would never have contemplated. When I arrived at the hotel where she was staying, she had just met some Kenyan government officials and had managed to get special invitations to a garden party at the State House the next afternoon.

And so, at 4 pm on Sept 5, 1965, with a special invitation from his Excellency Jomo Kenyatta, Sally and I attended a garden party at the State House in Mombasa. It was a gala affair, with elegantly dressed embassy bigwigs and Kenyan politicians. Hundreds of people attended, and when we sat down at a table to dine, there he was sitting almost exactly opposite from me, Jomo Kenyatta, the first president of Kenya.

For the next several hours we were entertained by dancers, singers, and acrobats, representing a spectrum of Kenya's different tribal groups. Between performances ranging from school choirs to Watusi dancers, we chatted with Kenyatta. He was friendly, genteel, and a stimulating conversationalist, asking us about, among other things, President Kennedy and American baseball.

Before coming to Africa I had done background reading, including the book *Something of Value* by Robert Ruark. In conversing with Kenyatta, I found it difficult to imagine that the gentle and friendly man across from me was the former leader of the Mau-Mau, a rebel who had taken the blood oath, later imprisoned for his "crimes." It wasn't until years later when I was less naive and better informed of some of the true facts regarding the Mau-Mau movement and Kenya's struggle for independence, that I became more sensitized to the relativistic nature of history, and how subjectively historical events are interpreted, recorded, and, accordingly, distorted. History is as the history writer views it.

18

Uganda

Leaving Mombasa, Sally and I returned to Nairobi, then briefly parted ways. After a day in Nairobi, I boarded a public bus and headed to Kampala, the capital of Uganda. The long trip through the Great Rift Valley was scenically dramatic, and on the way I struck up conversation with a Ugandan man in the seat in front of me. His name was John Semattire, and he worked at Mulago Hospital in Kampala, one of the largest and best equipped hospitals in East Africa at that time. After sleeping that night in a room at a cheap hotel, I spent the next two days at his invitation with his family, meeting his lovely wife and handsome young son, Kazibwe, afflicted with polio.

Several days later I rendezvoused with Sally and several other PCV's from Nigeria X, and we headed north from Kampala to Murchison Fall National Park, Uganda's largest national park. The park is bisected by the Nile, and in the 60's it was a common destination for travelers looking to witness its spectacular assemblage of wildlife. Entering the park, we passed a large yellow sign with the silhouette of an elephant on it, warning visitors that "elephants have the right of way." Inside the park we drove through lovely green savannah habitat, with vistas of long grass, scattered trees, and many large brown boulders.

Wait ... those weren't boulders, but elephants! In the 60's the park was home to hundreds of thousands of elephants, a truly amazing spectacle of wildlife abundance. Then came the terrible reign of Idi Amin. Uganda was wrenched apart by bloody civil war and the army, seeking moving targets for practice, trained their artillery on elephants. Thousands were slaughtered, and only now is the park's population slowly recovering.

Before finding lodging for the night, we visited Murchison Falls (Kabalega Falls), named for one of the past president's of Britain's Royal Geographical Society. At the world famous falls water originating from Lake Victoria thunders over a wide escarpment, or is forced through a seven meter gap in the rocks, and tumbles forty meters down to the river Nile. The water then flows towards Lake

Keoga and on to Lake Albert. The falls and surrounding countryside were beautiful and spectacular, especially viewed from the top, where the roiling, foaming water raged through the gorge and over the escarpment, with a thunderous roar to the Nile below.

When Sally and I arrived at park headquarters seeking accommodation for the night we discovered that the lodge, with its furnished rooms and modern bathroom facilities, had been entirely booked by two busloads of Texas tourists. We stayed, instead, at the nearby tent village, consisting of two rows of one, two, or four-person green canvas tents. Each tent was equipped with a cot, small bedside table, and a deck chair outside.

Shower and toilet facilities, located behind the tents, consisted of small circular huts with bamboo walls and thatched roofs. Inside there were pit toilets and a suspended water-filled metal bucket attached to a pull rope for showering.

I took a one-person tent, and Sally a tent nearby. As I was inside stowing my backpack, I found an object tucked into one of the corners of the tent. It was a plastic prescription bottle made out to a Mr. John Wayne. I later learned that the famous actor, and other members of the Hollywood film-making crew, had recently been in the park on location, filming scenes for the movie "*Hatari.*"

For guests staying at the tent village, evening supper was a simple affair, served at picnic tables in the open around a campfire beneath a canopy of stars. As we ate a packaged box supper and drank hot tea brewed over a wood fire, I queried the young British couple who were the managers.

"Today in the park we saw many elephants. What is the likelihood that they might decide to walk in the vicinity of our tents?" I asked.

"Very likely," the woman replied, "this area is right along one of their major travel routes."

Without thinking too deeply about the full implications of her remark, I retired to my tent. Several times, during the night, I wakened to relieve myself in the bamboo-walled, grass-thatched toilet and shower facility about ten yards away.

The next morning, at the first light of dawn, I was awakened by an unusual noise that I can only roughly describe as the sound of small bushes being uprooted from the ground. Bleary-eyed, I exited my tent and stood facing the first glimmers of light, from a sun not yet visible on the horizon. As my eyes adjusted, I was astounded to see at least six elephants slowly moving and foraging around and among the tents, including a large adult with big tusks only twenty feet away. I still have the photo capturing that moment, taken without the aid of a telephoto lens; the silhouette of the elephant fills the entire frame, with the yellow glow of dawn's light as a backdrop.

I called out as loudly as I dared to Sally. "Sally, get up, there's an elephant outside your tent." Seconds later she responded "What are you talking about … are you drunk?" When I insisted that there really were elephants near her tent, she emerged camera in hand and took one of the most memorable photos of her two years in Africa.

The presence of the elephants did not go unnoticed by some of the Texas tourists at the lodge about 500 yards away. They had gotten up early with all their camera paraphernalia to document the sunrise. They excitedly and loudly began to shout "Elephants, elephants" to their companions inside the hotel, and what had been a quiet moment for observation and reflection of one of nature's wonders was quickly transformed into chaos as the elephants began to stampede through the village. No tents containing human occupants, thankfully, were in the path of their retreat, but one of the bamboo toilet huts was tipped over and subsequently crushed by members of the herd, numbering over a dozen animals.

The day was one of perfect weather, sunny and mild, and after breakfast Sally and I, and several of the Texans, boarded one of the large boats available for rental trips up the Nile to a point about a mile from the base of Murchison Falls. In the 60's, during pre-civil war days when Ugandan tourism was booming, a boat trip up the Nile was the highlight of a visit to the park. We boarded a large motorized boat equipped with a sun canopy, and enough seats on either side to accommodate about a dozen passengers. One of the Texans was fully prepared to live the moment. She sat near the prow of the boat dressed in designer safari clothes, complete with pith helmet and veil. Around her neck hung two camera's and a pair of binoculars. In her hands she held a copy of *The While Nile* by Alan Moorhead. From her prow perch, as we traveled upriver towards the falls, she periodically glanced down at the open book. She never did any reading; like her garb and get-up, the book was all for show, to heighten the effect.

It was a half-day trip from the boat dock to the falls and back. As we traveled the Nile we passed swampy areas, extensive reed beds near shoreline, sandy beaches, and huge trees lining the river. Birds were numerous, including African fish eagles, carmine bee-eaters, kingfishers, and saddlebill and shoebill storks, but most impressive by far were the large numbers of crocodiles and hippopotamus, in the water and resting on the beaches.

During the trip a spectacular, yet horrific, event occurred. Many of the female hippopotamus in the water were accompanied by young calves, which stayed close to their mother's side. Crocodiles will not bother adult hippos, and are typically not foolhardy enough to attack a vulnerable young calf near its protective mother, but at one point in the outward journey the boat passed through a large group of hippo swimming in the water, separating a calf from its mother. Mother and baby were physically separated by the boat for only a minute at most, but in that short time an opportunistic croc seized the moment. I watched as the isolated calf swimming only several feet from our passing boat, suddenly disappeared from view. It happened so fast that all I saw was the hippo calf at the surface one second and gone the next, an eddy in the water's surface where the calf had been, and a portion of the disappearing tail of a large croc as it pulled the hapless calf under.

After spending several days at Murchison Falls National Park, Sally and I returned to Kampala. Everyone in our group was instructed to rendezvous at the Kampala municipal airport for the charter flight return to Ibadan. In spite of the fact that over a hundred PCV volunteers and staff persons had traveled in East Africa for several weeks, with individuals or small groups each going their separate ways, in some instances to remote and isolated locales, everyone showed up at the airport on the pre-determined day and time for the return trip to Nigeria.

19

Son of Sorrow, Son of Shame

The letter was emotion-charged, filled with pathos, and effusive in its outpouring of sympathy for the tragic misfortune that had befallen me. It was from Matthew, a student who frequently visited on weekends. It was written shortly after my return from East Africa, following the discovery of a second major theft of money from my home. The letter began:

> *"I could not believe my ears when I was hearing the recent catastrophe that has occurred in your life adventure. I am not particularly worried over the accusation or suspicion (a clear conscience fears no accusation) but I am grievously tormented over the situation this second theft has place you."*

Because he was one of several students who often visited me at home, I questioned Matthew regarding the theft, desperately trying to make sense of a situation that from its outset defied explanation. In his letter Matthew mentioned that the cost of enjoying the luxury of having friends is that one's life can become a nightmare of endless suspicion when the trust of friendship is betrayed. He was right. Although Matthew had visited around the time of the theft, I found it difficult to suspect him of thievery, and in his letter he assured me that he was not worried by what I might think of him ("a clear conscience fears no accusation"). I was confounded by my inability to clearly identify the culprit, and for the next several weeks my daily routine was laced with bitterness and suspicion.

It was mid-September 1965. I had been teaching at IBHS for sixteen months. Teaching had been accompanied by seemingly endless frustration. I was still having difficulties with the domineering principal, and issues of corruption and school mismanagement. The principal expected me to encourage Williams House boys to attend practice for the school's soccer team, but I couldn't take the task seriously. We were the only school that couldn't afford athletic uniforms or proper equipment, the only team with boys playing matches barefoot. How were their school fees being spent by the school, I wondered, as I contemplated the principal's big shiny black Cadillac parked in its reserved parking place? I continued to voice my opposition to the daily caning of students who broke school rules; I had grown weary of hearing whacked backsides and screaming boys heralding the beginning of each school day.

As science department head, I was exasperated trying to teach science without good equipment and no budget. Teaching biology according to a British syllabus and preparing students for the West African School Certificate (WASC) and General Certificate Examination (GCE) was difficult enough in a cultural context where science often clashed with native superstition, but to do so without working microscopes in biology, or with broken glassware and insufficient numbers of test tubes in chemistry seemed senseless. In addition, Nigeria's political climate was becoming increasing volatile and unstable, circumstances that would eventually precipitate the tragic Biafran war.

Having my personal life made difficult by major acts of theft in my home was the last thing I needed. Desperately seeking clues to solve the crime, and clear the cloud of suspicion hanging over me, I tried to recollect every neighbor or house guest I might have alienated or inadvertently offended. I could think of none. Lacking any focus or sense of where to begin unraveling the mystery, I carried out my teaching obligations routinely but without zeal, looking forward to weekends and vacations, and especially my return to the USA.

Had I known then what I learned later, I would have started my memory search for a solution to the thefts seven months earlier, soon after the beginning of the first term of school in January 1965.

It was the second day of the new term, and I was in the biology laboratory recording names in my class register. As I worked, a student entered and approached. I recognized him as a transfer student who had recently been admitted into one of the upper forms. He introduced himself as Segun. He told me that he only intended to remain at the school for one term, before leaving to study on his own in preparation for his GCE exams. After sharing a litany of personal life misfortunes, he asked me if I would personally help him with his studies. We talked for several minutes. Perhaps it was his age, the serious look on his face, or the emotional overtones and desperate nature of his appeal; whatever the reason, I agreed to help him in whatever way I could. He looked so much older than the other boys in class, probably older than myself. There I sat with an M.S. degree, advantaged and optimistic about my future, while he stood before me tall and awkward in the regulation school uniform. I was a graduate teacher, he a high school student. He seemed desperate in his hopes to pass the exams and "make something of his life." How could I refuse him?

I saw much of Segun after that. He came to my home frequently in the evenings, to read and study, while I prepared biology lessons. I never doubted his sincerity to learn, but had serious reservations about his academic abilities. He was in my biology class and had badly failed every quiz. He said it was because he never studied biology at his former school. When I questioned him he was reluctant to talk about his previous educational background, and as I came to know him better, it became clear that school, family, and other aspects of Segun's past, were secrets he did not intend to share with me.

As time passed he began to act more like a roomer than a guest. I valued my privacy and considered my home a cocoon of sanity, a private retreat. For nearly a year I had allowed a student, Rufus Obe, to stay with me when his family came upon hard times and were unable to pay his lodging in one of the school's boarding houses. I had two unused rooms in Adeyoola Chambers and offered to help the family, knowing Rufus to be a conscientious and promising student. He studied quietly in his room, and I barely knew in was in the house.

Segun's behavior, on the other hand, was overly familiar, almost brazen. I often became annoyed with him for entering the house without knocking, opening my desk drawers, or examining the contents of the refrigerator. But as time passed, I became more tolerant and accommodating. My insistence on courtesy, and at times solitude, probably made him think me strange, as he was part of a culture where the sharing of possession with friends is normally taken for granted. Our conversations were limited in scope. Much of the time he talked about Nigerian political corruption, or how he was mistreated and verbally abused by his classmates. I noticed that he kept apart from the other boys at school, a fact I attributed to his age and new surroundings.

When the school term ended we took a three day trip together, visiting the lovely coastal town of Badagry. Was it then—those first feelings that light was beginning to filter through the chinks in the cultural barrier separating us? We returned home to Ibadan, I to do more solo traveling before the beginning of the next school term, and Segun to a menial job. He told me he would no longer be attending IBHS, no money he said.

He continued to visit Adeyoola Chambers in the evenings. He arrived on his bicycle, sometimes just for a minute, sometimes for an hour or more, and almost always to complain about his sorry plight. Although he cautioned me about being too trusting with students and visitors, he moved about the house as though he were family. His behavior often confounded me, but I felt the bonds of under-standing broadening.

When he invited me to accompany him to Ijebu-Ode to visit his father, and see the festivities during the Moslem feast of Id al-Fitr, I was delighted and hap-pily accepted his invitation. During our visit with his father, the Oba of Owu, I remembered sensing something strange and troubling in their relationship, but thought little of it at the time.

Weeks passed, and from May through July I began to experience financial shortfalls. I was puzzled by the recurring monthly budget shortages because the Peace Corps subsistence salary had always been adequate for my needs. During my first year in Nigeria I lived frugally, always managing to save several pounds each month. After each bank visit I kept the spending money budgeted for the month locked in the small wooden cupboard in my bedroom. When I first arrived there had been two keys, but I could only account for one which I kept with me at all times. I have always been thrifty, but then I was much too casual about money and did not keep records of all my expenses, including monthly wages for my cook-steward and money I gave him for the weekly shopping. I attributed the money shortfalls to the fact that I was probably spending too much for provisions, even though my food was not purchased at the Western-style supermarket in the city, but from the less expensive open market and local native vendors.

I cautioned Moses to be frugal with the weekly food money. When that proved ineffective, during a two month period, I tightened the purse strings, lim-iting him to only one pound a week. He swiftly retaliated by serving me a steady diet of yam and beans. His strategy worked, and I increased his weekly food allot-ment, but even with strict budgeting money seemed to keep disappearing.

The possibility of theft had crossed my mind, yet if someone was periodically stealing money it would have to be someone in the household or a frequent visi-tor. The only people who could be involved were friends Ed and Helen, fellow house occupants Moses and Rufus, several Peace Corps friends who sometimes visited, and the few Nigerians like students Matthew, Musa, and Layiwola, or friends Abiodun and Segun, who often visited. All had my trust, and none seemed reasonable candidates.

In September 1965, soon after returning from my East Africa vacation, another money shortfall occurred. That was when the thought of a thief first seri-ously entered my mind. Although this was the second major money shortage I knew of, because of my casual attitude about money, other losses may have occurred but gone undetected. When I shared the facts with others there was a response of general disbelief and generous outpourings of sympathy, one of which was Matthew's letter. Many, like Matthew, said I was too naive and trusting. I was confused, unwilling to concede that the solution was explainable by theft. I lay awake at nights, my fertile imagination thinking up conceivable alternative explanations.

Could the driver ants have returned? Could they be raiding the locked cupboard at night, carrying away currency as I lay sleeping? Perhaps there existed some unusual West African insect, adept at camouflage or the art of hiding in the small cracks of wooden cupboards, with a dietary predilection for pound notes. No matter what scenario's emerged from those sleepless nights, evidence inexorably pointed to a thief, and when I collected money from the bank on a Friday to cover expenses for the month of October, I marked each note. When I checked the cupboard early on Sunday morning all the money was still there and undisturbed, but when I returned from school on Monday eleven pounds were missing. I was furious, and angrily confronted Moses.

"Moses, there is money missing from my bedroom."

"Oh, sir, I am very sorry sir."

"I am angry Moses, and I am holding you responsible. You have been careless."

"Sir, it is not my fault sir. I have housework to do and can not watch all the people who visit the house." My anger intensified.

"Moses, money is missing. It must have been stolen. This is the second big theft that I know of. Where were you today? Did you lock the house when you went to market?"

"Sir, I am very careful sir. I always lock the house when I leave. I am a good servant sir."

"But eleven pounds is missing. I know it was there yesterday. Did any strange people enter the house today?"

Moses was now upset, reacting with greater emotion to my accusations of dishonesty and disloyalty. "No sir, no strangers in the house while you were gone sir. Sir, please, I am blameless. I am honest, sir, please believe me."

We stood confronting one another in the kitchen. He continued to profess his honesty and loyalty, arguing that he had not been careless and let a stranger into the house that day. I could think of no suspicious persons in the house on Sunday, his day off. We were at stalemate. Knowing that a thief had successfully ripped me off once again in spite of all my precautions, I focused suspicions on the most likely culprit—Moses. I lost my temper, accused him of the theft, took his house keys, and told him to leave.

"You are making a terrible mistake sir," he cried, as he fell to his knees and began pleading and sobbing.

His show of deep and genuine emotion took me off guard. I suddenly became passive, shocked at my callousness and abrupt accusation. Moses had worked for me for nearly a year and never given me cause for complaint. His wife had recently died, leaving him with a son to support, and he desperately needed the job I was so quick to deny him. Not very convincingly, I'm sure, I tried to explain that I could see no other choice open to me. He was the only person who could have taken the money. He continued to plead with me, asserting his innocence, but after several more emotion-charged minutes I lost my temper again and angrily forced him out the door, locking it behind him. He remained on my doorstep for a long time, crying and pleading.

"I am innocent, sir. Please, have mercy. I have served you faithfully, and would never steal from you. Please sir, my child."

I remained unmoved, heartless and adamant. It had to be Moses. Who else could it be?

"Please sir. I beg you. I am innocent sir, you must believe me."

For two weeks after discharging Moses, I managed alone. Then, in early November, I acquired my last cook-steward, Joshua. I shared him with downstairs neighbors Ed and Helen, who were finishing their tour of duty and preparing to return to the States in several weeks time. I felt terrible about how I had treated Moses, but rationalized my meanness of spirit and the brutal manner in which I had dismissed him, by concluding that he could have been the only person doing the thieving, even though I had no proof.

On a Saturday morning, soon after hiring Joshua, and when he had gone to the market for provisions, one of my favorite students, Layiwola, was reading at the house when I left to go to school for a few hours. I returned to find an agitated Layiwola. "Segun was here to see you," he said, "and when he left he carried away two of your books beneath his shirt."

I was stunned. I had noticed books missing from my paperback library, but it had never occurred to me that they might have been stolen. I asked Layiwola to say nothing to anyone, and went to my bedroom to lie down. Before doing so, I checked the cupboard. Two more marked five pound notes were missing! Jumbled thoughts and memories reeled through my brain. Not Segun! Not the one Nigerian I had made such an extra effort to help, with whom I had traveled and shared memorable times.

I talked to Joshua, and he told me that Segun came to the house nearly every morning after I left for school. Reluctantly, I conspired with Joshua to set a trap.

On the next Monday morning, instead of leaving early for school as was my usual routine, I moved my motorcycle from the shed, and remained hiding behind the kitchen door. Soon Segun appeared. Joshua told him I was gone, let him in as planned, then returned to his ironing. I watched in disbelief as Segun brazenly opened my closed bedroom door and entered the room. Within a minute he reappeared and bid Joshua goodbye.

Quickly I ran to the locked cupboard in my bedroom, opened it with my key, and examined the marked money. No! A chill of anger and disillusionment overwhelmed me. Another twelve pounds was missing. Segun had the missing key. Segun was the thief! I quickly ran outside, but he had disappeared. I did not know where he was living and asked Joshua to try and locate his whereabouts while I was in school.

I remember that day vividly. Attending classes and teaching lessons was torture. Since arriving in Nigeria my values regarding time, efficiency and educational methods had undergone necessary and drastic revision. My faith in education as a solution to the world's ills and ailments had been endlessly challenged and shaken. Money orders and boxes of books mailed by family and friends to me at my IBHS address had never arrived. The personal science books I brought with me, and donated to the school on my arrival, had been stolen from the unsupervised library. Books published in Great Britain, to which the students were generally accustomed, were typically poorly illustrated. The American biology texts I donated, filled with illustrations and colorful photos, had proved too tempting.

As head of the science department the principal expected me to run an adequate science program, yet provided no money for necessary supplies. One month after arriving the Revolutionary Council of the Nigerian Youth Congress demanded the removal of all Peace Corps volunteers, accusing us of being trained spies and subversives. Three months after that most of the boarding students boycotted classes in protest of a six pence fine levied on each student by the headmaster for a broken electric meter for which no one took responsibility, and an all-school riot followed. During political protests later that year, the Nigerian army dispersed protestors on the school grounds by lobbing tear gas canisters near the classrooms, routing classes. I had alienated the principal by making it clear that I thought viciously caning students for minor infractions to be counter-productive. Frustrations and defeats had continually cropped up in the classroom and staffroom. But this was the last straw!

The last thing in the world I wanted to do at that moment was to attend class and teach Nigerian students that tomorrow might turn and steal from me. I wanted to escape from all things foreign, to jump on the next plane for the States. Somehow I managed to survive the day, and when school was over I rushed home. Shortly thereafter Joshua arrived, excited and breathless.

"Sir, I have located the house where Segun is living."

"Take me there," I said.

Within minutes a vigilante group of four—Joshua, Layiwola, friend and fellow Peace Corps volunteer Ed, and myself—were speeding towards the house on two Honda motorcycles. When we arrived we surrounded the house, stationing ourselves at all exits. What excitement! Within minutes people emerged from nearby houses and a crowd gathered; soon a policeman and the landlord were at the scene. For about fifteen minutes residents living in the house and neighborhood by-standers excitedly milled about the area. The atmosphere became increasingly tense and confused, with people yelling and shouting from both inside and outside the house.

Segun finally came out of the house, visibly shaken. When Ed, Joshua, Layiwola and I followed him up to his room, and I accused him of his treachery, he denied everything. Layiwola was especially upset, angrily yelling at Segun in Yoruba. I was unable to find any of the stolen marked money or my personal belongings, but his room had a new full-sized bed and a new mattress still in its plastic wrapping, obviously recent purchases. A heated discussion ensued with everyone shouting advice. I was hesitant to go through all the trouble and turmoil of pressing charges and going to court, and was feeling so miserable and perplexed that I began to care nothing about seeing justice done or guilty parties punished. All I wanted was my stolen money and possessions, and the opportunity to escape and be alone.

By now a large crowd of several hundred people had gathered. Most were curious and passive by-standers, but several men, perhaps friends or neighbors of Segun, were sending signals that they were unhappy with my presence. At my urging, the four of us left Segun, the policeman, the landlord, and the growing agitated crowd, and returned to Adeyoola Chambers. That evening, while home alone downing several bottles of Star beer, I decided to visit Segun's father, the Oba of Owu. I hoped he would know what to do.

Early the next morning I took a taxi to the lorry park, boarded a crowded mammy wagon, and made the fifty mile journey south to Ijebu-Ode. The Oba, remembering my previous visit, graciously welcomed me into his home. He had just returned from a ceremony and was in elegant native dress. He carried a fan and had beadwork around his neck. After several minutes I got up courage to discuss his son's situation, and explained the reasons for my visit. When I finished speaking he sat silent with his head down for several minutes, then looked up at me.

"I did not speak to you at length during your first visit," he began, speaking excellent English, "because Segun introduced you to me as his teacher. Although I was annoyed with him for being so presumptuous to visit me unannounced, I entertained both of you, out of respect to your presence. I am so sorry for what has happened, and for your losses."

He continued speaking.

"Segun attended secondary school for eleven years, and was a failure as a student. For one year he was not heard of. I drove him from my house when he nearly killed his younger brother. He stole things from others in the household, including his own family. I have disowned and disinherited him; he is no longer a son of mine, and I wish he had died years ago. He is a son of sorrow, a son of shame."

I was dumbstruck, speechless. Were the Oba and I talking about the same person? Was I so naive to be unaware of these negative aspects of Segun's character? Suddenly, confronted with a father's knowledge of his eldest son, I realized how woefully little I knew about Segun. The Oba promised that my money would be returned, and sympathized with me for being so completely duped and deceived. I sat in my chair, confused and feeling stupid. The day was getting late, and I told the Oba that I needed to leave to catch a bus back to Ibadan. As I turned in the doorway to bid him goodbye, I could see that he was weeping.

For weeks thereafter, I played the martyr role with bitter aplomb. I was curt and grouchy at school, suspicious of my Nigerian friends, cynical of the entire society. Ed and Helen had returned to the States, and I felt there was no one I could talk to. Fortunately, as the Christmas holidays approached, I returned to my senses. The fault, after all, was largely mine. I remembered my first solo trip into New York City, and how naively I had allowed someone to steal my wallet on a subway near Times Square. Would I have felt any differently if instead of West Africa I had gone to New Mexico, and had personal possessions stolen by a native American who had next to nothing compared to myself? In my hopes of quickly becoming a cross-cultural success story, I had let good intentions cloud good judgment. In my attempts to quickly assimilate aspects of African culture, I had tried to accomplish with Segun in a short time something which, for many persons, might require a lifetime. We were products of one world but two different cultures, and it now appeared that perhaps I had befriended a young man who was emotionally ill.

In my desire to be accepted and to accept, I had erroneously equated involvement with understanding. Stealing, like many other aspects of human behavior, is a relativistic act; its seriousness depends on the circumstances. While standing on my Adeyoola Chambers balcony months earlier, I witnessed several adolescent boys savagely beating another boy who had stolen a ball point pen. Later someone told me that the reason for their vicious retribution of hurt and public shame was not so much the act of stealing, but because the victim was someone poorer than the thief. Like the assembly-line worker who finds it easy to take pencils from the impersonal corporate entity, it is much easier to steal from strangers, or from those who can best afford it; a way of leveling out the disparities between rich and poor that existed in 1965, and persist to an even greater degree today.

After our confrontation on the day of the theft, I never saw Segun again. One of his older sisters and her husband visited me one evening in December. As she was leaving, she gave me a check for thirty-three pounds, the amount known stolen in the last three thefts.

Months passed, and no word from Segun. I became interested in his whereabouts and inquired. I learned that he had quit his job and left his room with only a few belongings. Then, on Feb. 16, 1966, two months before I was scheduled to leave Nigeria, I returned home late one night and found a large cardboard box sitting on my porch. It was filled with books, bed sheets, and articles of clothing, many of which I had not even realized were missing. Segun had been there. He had returned all of my stolen possessions. Inside the box was a pathetic and touching three-page letter of apology. The first sentence read "God has been wishing me to confess my sins to you, but Devil the Satan did not allow me."

Before leaving Nigeria I wrote Segun a reply letter. Within it I included his one request—my forgiveness. We are all brothers by virtue of our shared humanity, but as we enter the era of the global village it is important to recognize that cultural differences often set significant barriers to one's ability to transcend culture, and truly understand and be accepting of one another.

Now, forty years later, I not only more fully appreciate the differences that existed between Segun and me, but welcome the fact that such differences prevail. Today I remember my Nigerian acquaintances with fondness, not because of how alike we were as a consequence of our shared humanity, but because of our cultural differences. I still find it difficult to understand why Segun betrayed our friendship. Perhaps failed attempts to fully understand that which is foreign to our own experience is most significant if it induces us to isolate and insulate ourselves from the real world because of an unwillingness to accept the fact that others do not perceive reality through our eyes or interpret the human condition as we do. In any case, I am glad that Segun and I parted amicably and more than strangers.

20

Confessions of a Boarding House Master

When I first arrived at IBHS, the principal assigned me the responsibilities of a boarding house master. There were four "houses" in the block of buildings housing the boarding students, over 80% of the students at the school. I was housemaster for Williams House. I did not attack my responsibilities with zeal, largely because I felt totally unprepared and inadequate for the task. I submitted my required reports on time, and attempted to develop a spirit of cooperation among the boys, and to solve problems as they occurred. Because I was so involved with my teaching, and did not live on the school compound, many situations occurred in the boarding house that eluded me. By any standard of judgment, I was a failure as a boarding house master.

Other than teaching the 4th and 5th form biology and chemistry classes, being the nominal science department head, and stocking and staffing the school's dispensary, one of my major responsibilities was to oversee the production and publication of The Conqueror, the annual magazine of Williams House, whose motto was "Forward Ever, Backward Never." By January of 1966 my tenure as boarding house master was drawing to a close, and the principal had re-assigned the editorship for future editions of the magazine to two new teachers, Mr. Akinboye and Mr. Ogunsanya. Knowing myself to be a failed boarding house master in all other respects, I decided to relinquish the reins of editorship with a flourish, and to oversee the publication of the most impressive edition of The Conqueror that the school had ever seen.

Working with 5th form student magazine editors Tiko Alakpa and Olurotime Akitoye, I encouraged all Williams House boys to submit original articles and samples of their school work for the magazine. My request fell on deaf ears. Only a handful of students responded, and most of the submitted articles had to be returned because of sloppy writing, or rejected outright because of plagiarism.

Desperate to fill the magazine, and relentless in my pursuit of producing a literary masterpiece, I wrote two articles and submitted them under an assumed name—Ojogbon Iguniyanu. I did not anticipate that the students would catch me at my game, but of course everyone was wondering about the mysterious O. Iguniyanu. Was he a student at IBHS? If so, he was keeping a low profile, as no one knew him.

Eventually it came out that I had written the articles, in addition to the required House Master's Report at the beginning of the magazine. My report was a lengthy and presumptuous bit of prose that encouraged the boys to read widely, think deeply, and do their part for the future of mankind. Its cloying pretentiousness makes for unbearable reading, but I take comfort in knowing that everyone who read The Conqueror that year took no notice of it.

One of the two articles I wrote for the magazine, under the alias of mystery student O. Iguniyanu, concerned an aged beggar that I usually saw in a certain place on the side of the road near the barber shop where I went for haircuts. After my disastrous experience with the itinerant Yoruba barber, I patronized a barber that had experience cutting the hair of Europeans. His shop was located near Ibadan's city center. The students didn't like my story of the beggar, and chastised me for putting such a non-uplifting and somberly critical article in the magazine. I did so because I wanted them to think about the plight of the downtrodden and neglected, but they took it as a personal attack on their country.

THE BEGGAR

Whenever I went into the city center last year I saw him sitting alone by a stone wall at the side of the road. He wore a soiled white garment and a ragged headpiece, and his head was always lowered as though he were asleep. He appeared to be about sixty years old, and he was always there beneath the silk cotton tree, regardless of the weather or the time of day.

I never learned his name, nor lingered as I passed him by. Whenever I saw him I felt as though I should stop, but instead I moved on quickly and took little notice. I think I would have been embarrassed, perhaps ashamed, if I had approached close to him, and then done nothing to help. I did often stop and observe him from a distance, but even this was awkward, and I always soon left to go on my way. Every time I chanced his way I found him huddling close to the wall, and always in the same place. Perhaps he slept there, I cannot be sure.

His right hand clutched a wooden staff which helped him remain in an upright position. By his side was a small enameled metal bowl. People carefully passed around him, and sometimes dropped money in the bowl. He kept his right leg tucked out of the way. His left leg, swollen, sore-covered, and quite life-less, was thrust out in front of him. As I recollect all this now, I realize that I have no impression of his face. All that I remember is his lonely huddled form and his infected leg, tormented by clouds of buzzing flies.

Yesterday I traveled to the city for the first time in several months. As I passed the silk cotton tree I looked for the old man, but he wasn't there. A steady stream of people passed the wall, and but for the absence of his huddled form, all seemed the same as before.

I tell you this. I never knew the old man. I never uttered a word to him. I never approached to greet him, or to drop a coin in his bowl. Perhaps he was con-tent to spend his days sleeping by the wall; perhaps, I tell myself, entering into his life would only have disturbed him. Before, those many times when I saw him, I remember feeling shame, and yes, I admit it, disgust. Disgust not so much for the old man and his infected leg, but for the inadequacies of the human condition which relegated him to his circumstance in life.

Today I passed the wall again. I stopped by the place where he used to sleep away his days. I cannot explain it adequately in words, but I felt an emptiness, a feeling of loss. I missed him for not being there.

21

Tribalism Triumphs, Rumblings of War

In October of 1965, general elections were held in the Western Region. Political tensions had been running high since December of 1964 when the first national elections since independence in 1960 were held. At that time the NNDP (Nigerian National Democratic Party), the party holding power in the West, had aligned itself with the NPC party of the Northern Region. This precipitated a shifting of allegiances, and led to the Eastern Region further isolating itself from the other regions. During the October elections Chief Samuel L. Akintola and the NNDP party claimed victory and retained power in the Western Region, amidst cries of fraud and election rigging. With the popular opposition leader of the Action Group party, Obafemi Awolowo, incarcerated in Calabar prison, the defeated opposition candidate and current Action Group leader, Adegbenro, claimed election rigging. Over one hundred and sixty persons in the Western Region died in election strife, and for several days tensions in Ibadan were high. Action Group supporters, seeking political revenge, periodically engaged in rioting, looting, house burning, and murder.

Awolowo's house, and Action Group political headquarters, were immediately next to the IBHS compound, and so the situation in the Oke-Ado area of Ibadan was especially tense. Rogues and thugs, seeking asylum in the area, created tension and strife at the school. For several successive days hundreds of Action Group supporters and market women, angered by restrictions placed on the gathering of crowds in the markets, assembled on the school grounds. They confronted the army and the police, which had surrounded both Awolowo's headquarters and the school. On three successive days the army lobbed tear gas canisters towards the phalanx of market women, nearly all carrying infants on their backs. The drifting gas on the school grounds effectively dispersed the mobs, and routed classes. One day, my biology class was abruptly terminated when tanks rumbled across the playing field and clouds of tear gas drifted in the classroom windows.

"The tanks are coming," several students yelled, as I commenced a review of the parts of a flower. With no warning, we heard explosions, and the screams of the market women, scattering in all directions, as an acrid smoke cloud entered the classroom. Hooray for the Nigerian army. With their tanks and tear gas, they showed those defenseless women and infants a thing or too.

After Adegbenro's arrest turmoil in the school area settled down but Ijebu Bypass, the main road leading to the school, remained blocked off. For several weeks I passed through police barriers in order to get to work.

December 1965 arrived, and the 5th form students were preparing for final exams. As the teacher it was my responsibility to administer the WASC exams to the 5th form boys in my chemistry and biology classes. As had happened before, one year earlier, I was required to gather the materials required for the practical component of the biology exam. This time I needed to have a mosquito with undamaged mouthparts, and a large ripe or nearly ripe mango, for each of the students sitting for the exam, a total of forty boys. The practical exam questions asked the students to draw a labeled sketch of a female mosquitoe's piercing and sucking mouthparts, and a labeled sketch of a cross-section through a mango fruit, showing the large centrally located seed containing the embryo plant. Collecting the mangos was relatively simple. I quickly located a mango tree with ripe dangling fruits on low hanging branches. Collecting the mosquitoes was the real challenge. Each night, for a week, I searched the walls and ceilings of Adeyoola Chambers, carefully capturing the insects in a vial containing isopropyl alcohol, exercising caution so as not to mangle their mouthparts.

When the exams were over, still upset about the thefts and Segun's betrayal of our friendship, I was ready for some R and R. The Christmas school vacation was approaching, and I had no desire to spend the holidays alone in Ibadan. The school had recently hosted a going away party for friends Ed and Helen, and they were now back home in Maryland. Their hard-working and honest cook-steward Joshua, a member of the Efik tribe from Calabar in the Eastern Region, was now working fulltime as my cook-steward. As I had seen much of Nigeria with the exception of the Northern Region, I made tentative plans for a two week trip to the north. In response to a written query, I received an invitation from the Nigerian Institute for Trypanosomiasis Research, located in Vom on the Jos plateau, to assist researchers at the laboratories there. I planned to work there for seven days, then travel further north. I told Joshua I would be gone for several weeks, then left Ibadan in a lorry hauling a load of plantains.

I arrived in Vom shortly after my 26th birthday, on January 2, 1966. The director of the institute, a Dr. Godfrey, provided me room and board at Vom's catering rest house, and gave me a quick orientation to the laboratory. After explaining the research protocol expected of me, he abruptly left Vom and the institute for his vacation, leaving me to work largely on my own.

The institute was engaged in research to understand why some cattle breeds were more resistant than others to the trypanosome causing sleeping sickness. The long term goal of the research was to develop, through selective breeding, better adapted cattle strains for protein-starved West Africa that were less susceptible to the protozoan parasite causing the disease. For the week I was there, working alone and unsupervised in their large well-equipped laboratory, I carried out specific and technical research protocols, the details of which I have long since forgotten. I have only two clear recollections of my week at the Institute; I saw many different varieties of cattle, some frightfully emaciated, with varying resistance to the trypanosome parasite, and I broke several pieces of expensive laboratory glassware.

Leaving Dr. Godfrey a brief report of the work I had accomplished at the Institute, I left Vom in a crowded mammy wagon, traveling to Jos. From Jos I headed north to Zaria, to visit a friend and another Nigeria X PCV, Margaret, teaching chemistry at Ahmadu Bello University. Several days later I went to a lorry park and found a driver willing to take me to the far northern city of Kano. The one hundred mile trip was a hot, dusty, bumpy ride, uncomfortably lying in the back of the lorry on top of a pile of yams and bagged food goods.

I arrived at a lorry park in Kano on Saturday, January 15, 1966. The day was hot, with blue cloudless skies, and waves of heat rising from the surrounding arid sub-Sahara. After orienting myself to new and strange surroundings, I spent several hours roaming about in the Old City area, taking pictures of women at the dye pits and traders in the market. In the distance I could see huge Giza-like pyramids, many stories tall, composed of thousands of bags of groundnuts. As I was making my way to the Peace Corps hostel in the late afternoon for a much needed rest, I suddenly saw hundreds of people running down the street ahead of me, all shouting words in the Hausa language that I didn't understand. The streets quickly became a beehive of activity; people excitedly running and shouting, shopkeepers hastily shutting down their businesses. In the distance I heard gunfire.

As soon as I heard the guns, amidst people excitedly running in all directions, I began speedwalking in the direction of the hostel. Once inside, I turned on a radio and learned that the civilian government had been overthrown in a military coup staged mainly by junior Igbo (Ibo) army officers from the Eastern Region. I did not realize it at the time, but the coup was the first of a series of consecutive political conflicts that precipitated an unfolding scenario of tragic events. The ripple effects, as they played out, included further killings, the massacre of thousands of Igbos by Northerners, the secession of the Eastern Region from the rest of the country, and, finally, the bloody Biafran War which lasted from July 1967 to January 1970. The coup, and its violent aftermath, shattered the image of Nigeria as black Africa's beacon of stability and most promising showcase of democracy.

Although Kano was the Northern Region's largest city, most of the turmoil in the north occurred in the capital city of Kaduna, and in Sokoto, the region's religious center. Rebel troops mainly consolidated their positions in Kaduna, where several high-ranking Muslim army officers loyal to the government were killed. Elsewhere in Kaduna, rebels killed the northern Premier Sir Ahmadu Bello and his wife as they lay in their beds, then burned the home. Ahmadu Bello, the Sardauna (Sultan) of Sokoto, represented the spiritual head of Islam in the country. His death inflamed the passions of northern Hausa Moslems against the rebels, most of whom were eastern Igbo Christians.

In Lagos, the internationally respected Prime Minister, Sir Abubakar Tafawa Balewa, also a northerner, along with his next door neighbor, Finance Minister Chief Festus Okotie-Eboh, were kidnapped, and presumably killed. Their bodies were later found in shallow graves, along with the bullet-ridden bodies of several high ranking army officers.

And in Ibadan, the Premier of the Western Region, Chief Samuel L. Akintola, who had been returned to power in the elections of October 1965, blatantly rigged by his appointed officials, was overwhelmed at his home in Ibadan by young rebel army officers and killed. Poor Akintola. How proudly he had posed with us for our group picture on the steps of Government House in Ibadan shortly after our arrival sixteen months earlier.

Following the coup, power was transferred to the General Commander of the Army, Major-General Aguiyi-Ironsi, an Igbo from the Eastern Region. Aguiyi-Ironsi had been trained at Sandhurst, Britain's West Point equivalent. He suspended the offices of the prime minister and the president, and established military rule. The official President of Nigeria, Nnamdi Azikiwe, was out of the country at the time of the coup, recovering in a London clinic after an operation for a lung infection.

For the next several days I remained in the Kano Peace Corps hostel, living off peanut butter sandwiches, staying inside and off the streets. I was alone except for two Hausa hostel workers that occasionally appeared to sweep the floors. They spoke no English, and I had no idea what conditions were like elsewhere in the city. I telephoned the Peace Corps office to inform them of my whereabouts in the event of escalations in the conflict, but they never called back. News reports on the radio were spotty and often conflicting. After several days of hearing no word from anyone, I decided it was time to leave Kano.

I walked to the train station and purchased a second class ticket for the long ride south to Ibadan. The train was overcrowded. As far as I could determine I was the only foreigner on board. I shared a small compartment with fourteen other people, all Nigerians, including a woman with five young children and a small flock of chickens. On the second day of the trip she cooked one of the chickens in a cooking pot on the wooden floor of our train compartment.

As the train slowly traveled the 625-mile trip south from Kano to Kaduna, Minna, Jebba, Ilorin, Oshogbo, and finally Ibadan, I saw occasional evidence of burned buildings and civilian unrest. From the train windows the presence of army vehicles and personnel were much in evidence, but considering the circumstances surrounding the recent murder of the Sardauna of Sokoto, the Muslim spiritual leader, the villages and countryside of the north seemed eerily calm. At no time during the nearly three day trip did I feel my safety in any jeopardy.

When I arrived home in Ibadan, a six page memorandum from the Peace Corps director of the Western Region, dated January 14, 1966, awaited me in my mail. The memorandum "A Guide for Emergency Situations" outlined instructions to be followed in the event of a region-wide emergency necessitating a rapid withdrawal of volunteers from the country. In general, the document encouraged PCV's to remain where they were in the event of most emergency situations, and to prepare for such a circumstance by having adequate amounts of non-perishable food goods, drinking water, and a reserve supply of money in small denominations. In the event of a necessary physical evacuation from the country, all volunteers in Ibadan were instructed to gather at Peace Corps headquarters located in the city.

Volunteers living in other parts and provinces of the Western Region were given specific instructions where to go; for example, all volunteers in Ijebu province were instructed to gather at Adeola Odutola Comprehensive School, and await transport by Peace Corps vans to Lagos or some other evacuation center. The memorandum also provided specific information about green alerts and red alerts and included a listing of hospitals where we could seek sanctuary, or be of some assistance, in the event of substantial violence and injuries resulting from a conflict situation.

In spite of the ominous tone of the memorandum, for the remainder of my time in Nigeria the political climate in Ibadan remained calm. It was only after I left Nigeria on April 26, 1966 that conflict re-surfaced. The resumption of hostilities eventually led to the Biafran War, in large measure a tribal conflict between eastern Christian Igbos and northern Hausa Moslems.

War is brutal and indiscriminating. Caught up in the Biafran conflict were many unwilling participants, including the Ogoni people of the Niger delta. The Ogoni, along with other small tribes like the Itsekeri, Ijaw, and Urhobo, are one of the smaller tribes comprising the 250 or so tribes in Nigeria. Unfortunately for the Ogoni, their homeland lies above a large portion of Nigeria's oil reserves in the oil rich Niger delta, a region about as large as the country of Scotland. What was once a rural community of farmers and fisherman in the 60's, is now a nightmarish landscape criss-crossed by 4,500 miles of pipelines, creeks poisoned by oil spillage, air reeking of sulfur fumes, and night skies illuminated by perpetually burning gas flares.

For my last six months in Ibadan, frustrated by conditions at IBHS, I volunteered to teach a Higher School Certificate biology class to women students at Saint Theresa's College. I was motivated, in part, by a desire to teach advanced biology and to have some experience teaching women students. When I finished work at 3 pm at IBHS, I traveled several miles down busy Ijebu Bye-Pass to St. Theresa's, a mission college, administered by Missionary Sisters of our Lady of Apostles, headquartered in Cork, Ireland. St. Theresa's had an expansive walled compound, and when I entered its sanctuary through the entrance gates from the noisy congested highway I always experienced a rejuvenating feeling of calm and relief.

It was like entering paradise. The long winding road from the main gates to the school buildings was lined by lovely red-flowered flamboyant trees and multicolored crotons. The trees, grottos, gardens, open vistas of well maintained lawn, and idyllic atmosphere of order and peace, seemed a garden of green tranquility, an oasis of pastoral serenity, separate and apart from the crowded confusion beyond its walls. At the start of each school day, the girls and young women marched in orderly fashion from the assembly hall to their respective classes, and the school's educational mission proceeded without interruption. No classrooms without teachers, no unattended students, no canings, no attempts to teach science laboratories with broken equipment or a lack of supplies—it was a refreshing change from Ibadan Boys High School.

There were twelve women in my class, about half of them Igbos from eastern Nigeria. All were good students, and many were planning to continue their education at a university. One of the Igbo women, Grace, was a shining light, an articulate academic high achiever, and an extremely attractive woman. After graduating from St. Theresa's, she went to Spain to pursue graduate studies.

I was fascinated by the elaborate plaiting of the women's hair styles. One day I asked Grace if she would consult with her classmates over the weekend and come to school on Monday, each with a different plaiting pattern. The women obliged, some spending over six hours plaiting their hair in preparation for the hair show. After class ended I took a group photo, then asked each girl to pose for me by the blooming hibiscus bushes outside the classroom so that I could photo-document their hair creations. The impromptu photo shoot was accompanied by much laughing and good humor.

While working at the college I became good friends with one of the sisters, Mary Majella McCarron, originally from county Mayo, Ireland. We were both about the same age. We frequently had tea together, discussing teaching and a wide variety of social and political issues. On two occasions she visited me at Adeyoola Chambers.

By early 1966 I was in correspondence with graduate schools, planning to begin PhD work at either Michigan State University or the University of Oklahoma. Both had accepted me and offered financial assistance in the form of NSF fellowships or research assistantships. In order that my last months in Africa not be too restful, perverse providence intervened to keep life unsettled. On January 30, the two locked motorcycles, mine and the one left by Ed, were stolen from the shed. In accordance with new austerity measures, the Peace Corps told me they would not be replaced. For my last three months in Nigeria I walked the four miles to and from IBHS each day, arriving for classes tired, and usually overheated and sweating. To get to St. Theresa's after finishing work at IBHS, I traveled by taxi or bus.

Traveling in Nigeria in early 1966 was risky. One day Sister Majella invited me to accompany two of the other St. Theresa sisters and herself to Benin on business. The sisters knew several honest Yoruba men living in Ibadan that were good drivers, and hired one of them to drive the four of us to Benin early in the morning, and return with us later in the day before dark. Although lawlessness was increasing throughout the country, the sisters assumed that travel during the daylight hours on a main road would pose few risks. The trip was without incident until we approached a bridge outside Benin at about noon on a little traveled section of the main highway. Two men emerged from the trees roadside about five hundred yards in front of us, dragging a large tree limb. They dropped it in the road, then ran off as our car slowed to a stop.

Immediately, seven rough-looking thugs, carrying rifles and machetes, emerged from underneath the bridge and ran in our direction. Brandishing their weapons, they surrounded the car in a threatening manner. One began arguing with the driver, as the others looked at us menacingly through the closed windows. After several minutes of arguing with the driver and among themselves, one man, the apparent ring leader, motioned for the driver to proceed ahead, as others removed the tree branch blocking our way. It was a frightening encounter. Were it not for the fact that I was traveling with nuns, I feel certain I would have been robbed or worse.

On Feb. 3, 1966 I received a memorandum from Alice O'Grady, the Peace Corps deputy director for the Western Region in Ibadan. The memo asked me to give a full report of the theft of Hondas WAL 117 and WAJ 886, and to inform her what action had been taken by the police. I could only tell her that they had been stolen from the shed adjacent to the house by persons unknown, and that the police had done nothing. The bikes were never recovered.

On February 16, 1966, I received a letter from David Elliott, the Peace Corps director in Nigeria. It described my volunteer service in the Peace Corps and read as follows:

"Mr. Sandford has been serving satisfactorily as a Peace Corps Volunteer since May, 1964. Before leaving the United States he successfully completed an intensive three month training program at Columbia Teachers Training University, New York.

He is responsible to the Ministry of Education of the Western Region of Nigeria and works for the Ministry in the capacity of Education Officer. He teaches Biology, Chemistry, and General Science. He is instructing 300 students a total of 24 hours per week at the Ibadan Boys High School in Ibadan, where he is one of 16 faculty members.

Additionally, as part of his school duties, he works as a house master, head of Science Society, chairman of Science Department, and School Dispensarian. Also, during his tour of duty during school vacation periods, he worked at the Oluyole Cheshire home, worked as a swimming instructor in a day-camp program, and assisted in the laboratory at the Nigerian Institute for Trypanosomiasis Research"

The letter omitted references to my teaching at St. Theresa's, probably because Peace Corps headquarters was unaware of the volunteer work I was doing there. Soon after receiving the letter, I had an unexpected visit from an official from Peace Corps Washington.

The Biafran War

On July 29, 1966, during a second military coup, Aguiyi-Ironsi was killed by northern troops, and Col. Yakubu Gowon assumed power. This choice was unacceptable to many Igbos, setting in motion events that tore Nigeria apart with yet more massacres and killings. Later in the year, Muslim Hausas killed hundreds of Christian Igbos in the east, many of whom had been driven from the north. From their refuge in the Eastern Region, Igbos, under the leadership of Colonel Chukwuemeka Ojukwu, had earlier decided to secede from the rest of Nigeria, taking most of the area containing the country's oil reserves with them. They called the new state the Republic of Biafra.

The two and a half year long Biafra War ended in January 1970 when Biafra surrendered to the Federal Government. As many as two million Nigerians died. The civil war mainly involved Hausa Moslems from the Northern Region and Igbo Christians in the seceding Eastern Region. The Yorubas that predominated in the Western Region, practicing either Islam, Christianity, or animism and other traditional ways of worship, remained largely uninvolved. Although the Biafran War ended in 1970, continual strife remains in Nigeria to the present between fundamentalist Muslims and Christians over the spread of repressive Islamic law ("sharia") in the largely Muslim north. This tribal and religious based discord threatens the stability of the country.

The negative consequences of an oil economy to the Ogoni, and the martyrdom of Ken Saro-Wiwa

Since the mid 1950's much of Ogoniland has been ruined by the industrial pollution accompanying oil extraction by international oil companies, Shell Oil in particular. A major spokesperson for his Ogoni people was the writer and ecological activist Ken Saro-Wiwa. He protested the desecration of his homeland and demanded compensation from Shell Oil and the Nigerian government, whose military leaders have pocketed millions to their own private purses from oil revenues, whereas local communities like the Ogoni have seen few economic returns, and must live in the destroyed landscapes that greed creates.

Ken Saro-Wiwa was a charismatic spokesperson and accomplished writer, an advocate of creative non-violence, and a man of courage and moral conviction. His endless campaigning against the devastation created in his homeland and that of the Ogoni people, by oil companies like Shell and Chevron, eventually led to his imprisonment for a year as an instigator of social unrest and an "enemy of the state" by the Nigerian federal government.

On Nov. 10, 1995, despite pleas for clemency by people from around the world, including Nelson Mandela and Nigerian writer and Nobel Laureate Wole Soyinka, Ken Saro-Wiwa, and eight other Ogoni colleagues, were executed by hanging on the orders of General Sani Abacha, the military leader of Nigeria at the time. The shameful and heinous murder of an innocent man by the Nigerian government did not go unnoticed by the world. Saro-Wiwa's martyrdom to the temple of greed and corruption surrounding the oil industry has become a beacon for others worldwide who struggle for environmental and social justice.

Whatever happened to Sister Majella?

Sister Majella is now (as of 2007) back in Ireland, pursuing yet another master's degree. She is actively involved in social justice issues for local communities negatively impacted by the actions of oil multinationals. By testifying at public hearings, giving radio and TV interviews, and helping maintain a website, she has become a leading spokesperson for MOSOP (Movement for the Survival of the Ogoni People), informing the naive public about the insidious activities of multinational oil companies in general, and the Shell Oil Company in particular, in the Niger Delta region of Nigeria, and elsewhere in the world. Companies like Shell Oil reap huge economic gains at the expense of local people, who see almost no economic benefits and are forced to live with the environmental destruction that comes with oil extraction, and the pollution that follows from leaking pipelines. We have continued to correspond since our days together in Ibadan, and I have visited her four times since during visits to Ireland and the UK.

22

A Visitor from Washington

One late Saturday afternoon I was sitting at my kitchen table devouring a fresh tropical fruit salad of banana, mango, pineapple and papaya, when I heard knocking on my back door. Opening the door, I confronted a tall, slender, well dressed woman with dark hair and glasses.

"Mr. Sandford?"

"Yes," I said, inviting her inside.

She introduced herself, then proceeded to inform me that she was from the Peace Corps office in Washington D.C. She was visiting Nigeria for a few days to meet with a selected sample of volunteers. The purpose of her visit was to evaluate the circumstances of volunteers, specifically with reference to living conditions and accessibility to certain amenities. Peace Corps officials in Washington, it seemed, believed that many volunteers were living too luxuriously, not presenting the austere atypical American image they wanted conveyed. The woman was pleasant enough, and I sympathized with the usefulness of official on-site visits and periodic evaluations, but I became somewhat disturbed when the conversation soon shifted from the realm of philosophical generalities to rude specifics. After several minutes of conventional pleasantries, the real reason behind her visit became clear.

"We've been evaluating the circumstances of volunteers in the field," she said, "and are considering the implementation of certain policy decisions."

"Oh?," I said.

"Yes. We are thinking that some volunteers are experiencing living standards and circumstances that we do not consider altogether desirable."

"Such as?" I queried.

"Well, to be precise, we are re-evaluating the necessity of refrigerators?"

"What?"

"Refrigerators," she reiterated. "We are not certain that the issuing of refrigerators is a necessity for successful volunteer service."

"But this is a tropical country. Food spoils quickly here," I replied.

I was anticipating perhaps some mention of the personal use of school vehicles, unnecessarily extravagant housing, or televisions. But refrigerators? I commenced to share some of my concerns.

"I really don't think a policy of not issuing refrigerators to volunteers is realistic. I certainly wouldn't appreciate having my refrigerator hauled away in the name of austerity, or to help promulgate the image of Peace Corps."

She had declined my offer of a seat when first arriving and remained standing in my kitchen, her body language and facial expression indicating a willingness to listen to what I might say. I continued.

"It's hard enough for the Nigerian teachers at my school to understand why I walk several miles to school each morning or, before it was stolen, came by motorcycle. Most of them arrive by taxi or drive their own cars."

She nodded sympathetically and I continued.

"It seems unnecessarily extreme, even ludicrous, to confiscate refrigerators. It's difficult enough to cope with the problems of teaching, and all the other activities and obligations associated with working in a tropical country. My Nigerian colleagues are intelligent. They know how the life style and work of Peace Corps volunteers differs from that of U.S. embassy officials, living comfortably as they do, and sequestered away as they are, in the exclusive Little America settlement in the best part of town."

"So you don't think it would be good policy to discontinue the use of refrigerators?" she asked.

"No, I don't. I think it would be stupid. I didn't come here expecting to live a life of luxury. I don't want it. I can accept simple living, even some hardship. But why facilitate the inefficiency that would come with food wastage and the risk of food poisoning? Isn't my job important enough not to risk compromising my health or throwing up unnecessary challenges to living day by day? Do the people at the Africa desk in Washington know what's it like to try and effectively teach in the heat and humidity of the disease-ridden tropics?"

Silence. I plunged on.

"And we are here to teach aren't we? How can removing our refrigerators possibly contribute to an improvement in our performance? The Nigerian teachers I work with all have refrigerators. I can assure you that removing my refrigerator will not improve my status in their eyes. It will only serve to call into question the sanity of Peace Corps Washington."

She seemed sympathetic to my words and the sincerity of my appeal, which had become increasingly emotional. We parted amicably, and she left to continue her survey with other volunteers before returning to Washington.

As early as March 1965, memo's had been circulating among Peace Corps officials about the "vehicle situation" for PCV's in Nigeria. Administrators had concluded that Hondas were not necessary, except in highly unusual situations involving volunteers in remote locations where public transport was unavailable. Personal vehicles, it seems, were not contributing to job performance, nor were they deemed compatible with the overall purpose or image that the Peace Corps wanted to convey. Honda confiscations began later in the year. Following the woman's visit, I heard reports of volunteers whose motorcycles were taken away in the name of austerity or involuntary simplicity, but I never heard of a confiscated refrigerator.

23

Visit to a Juju Man

I worked especially hard at my teaching during my last months at IBHS. At the beginning of my last term, the 5th form students were preparing to sit for their GCE and WASC exams in December 1966. I had taught these students most of the biology they had learned, and I knew I would not be their teacher in the final months before they sat for the exam. I knew how important it was for their future to pass their exams, and hopefully to pass with distinction. I spent much of the term helping them prepare by carefully reviewing all of the required biology syllabus, repeatedly testing them with mock written exams and laboratory practical exercises. IBHS students had an abysmally poor record of passing grades on the exams. I wanted the students to do especially well on the biology and chemistry exams, both for their future, and as some slight confirmation to myself that my efforts had actually made a difference.

Teaching science according to a British syllabus in a culture replete with superstitious notions and animistic beliefs was not without frustrations. The Yorubas put much faith in the power of talismans, charms, curses, and the efficacy of witch doctors (native healers) or "juju" men. At school I frequently overheard boys talking about unusual and fantastical biological happenings in their villages. During class periods, students often queried me about people dying from a curse, or women who could turn into birds, or give birth to turtles. Almost every Ibadan native market had juju stalls where it was possible to buy shrunken monkey heads, animal bones, desiccated animal body parts, whole dried rats, herbal remedies, magical potions, or fetishes to ward off evil spirits, or place curses on an enemy.

One day in class, after spending several weeks thoroughly (I thought!) reviewing material on sexual reproduction and the anatomy and physiology of the human reproductive system, I asked for questions. A boy, Waheed, raised his hand. "Mr. Sandford, sir, a woman in my village gave birth to a goat. Can you explain sir?"

I stood at the blackboard stunned and speechless, feeling the blood draining from my face. My heart sank as if a heap of sand within me. I felt like a deflated balloon, void of spirit. I stood staring out at my students, preparing to take the rigorous GCE exam administered by Cambridge University in England, one of the most important tests they would ever take in their entire lives. Had my thorough coverage of the subject matter required by the syllabus, including the workings of the human reproductive system, all been in vain? Had my work in Nigeria as a science teacher made any kind of meaningful difference? What were the long-term consequences of teaching modern science in a society so seeped in superstition, so accepting of animism? Were things really as hopeless as I sensed they were at that moment?

As a science teacher, I had continually experienced dilemma's relating to the conflict between empiricism and superstition, when dealing with explanations of occurrences in the natural world. Soon after arriving in Nigeria I read a report in the Lagos Daily Times recounting the breaking off of a limb from the traditional twin Olobun tree in the middle of Lagos during a storm. The incident had brought thousands of Nigerians to the scene to view the broken limb beneath the mystical tree. I kept the newspaper article in my journal to remind me, as a science teacher, of the challenges I faced. According to the newspaper account, some people thought that the limb had broken off because it was the rainy season and the unusually heavy downpour the previous day had placed additional weight and stress on the large branch. Most people, however, were convinced the limb snapped off because the tree goddess had not been appeased.

Unwilling to let the irrationality of superstitious belief prevail over the empirical approach of the scientific method, if only in my one small insignificant classroom at IBHS, I decided to confront the issue head-on. I responded to Waheed's question, informing the class that it was biologically impossible for a human woman to give birth to a goat. Then, I asked the students to give me the name of one of the best juju men in Ibadan. The students waxed enthusiastic about one particular man, a famous juju man and traditional healer, who lived in a small village outside the city.

Several days later I paid him a visit. Several students accompanied me to his house in a taxi, and waited with me outside as a curious crowd from the village quickly gathered. His house was small and typical of the Yoruba, consisting of red clay walls, dirt floor, and sheet metal roof. The students entered and conferred with the man in private. Eventually he came to the door, requesting in pidgin English that I enter alone.

Once inside the dim interior of his small two-roomed house, he beckoned me to sit on a small wooden footstool across from him. We sat facing one another, separated by a small dust-covered wooden table. He nodded at me, adjusted the sleeves of his soiled cream-colored sapara, then commenced his spiel. I sat quietly, watching his hand movements, and listening to his largely unintelligible words and non-verbal vocalizations. As I sat uncomfortably on the small, low, stool, my knees almost touching my chin, I looked about the room, intrigued and impressed by the arsenal of potions, powders, feathers, bones, skulls, dried plant material, and mummified animal body parts, displayed in dusty jars, boxes, bags, bowls and gourds on the shelves lining the wall behind him.

Towards the end of his "performance," which lasted several minutes, and included incantations, chanting, and trancelike states, he removed a metallic looking powder from a bottle, and one or more materials that I couldn't identify from a gourd, then ceremoniously placed them together in a piece of newspaper. Mumbling a few words in Yoruba, he then crushed up the paper and dropped it in a metal bucket by his feet. Seconds later there was a "whoosh" sound, and a dramatic flash of light, as the paper burst into flame. I responded with what I hoped was an appropriate display of awe at the amazing occurrence. He then reached under the table and produced a simple cloth charm guaranteed to protect me from all danger while traveling. He told me to take the amulet with me wherever I went and charged me three Nigerian pounds.

The next week I reported back to the students in my biology class about my visit, sharing with them my impressions of our meeting, and the juju man's theatrical performance. Although I was unable to give an exact explanation for the dramatic flash of light and fire at the finale, I explained to them how finely powdered metals like iron oxide, aluminum, or magnesium, when mixed with fine organic materials like grain dust or organic liquids like glycerol, can ignite and cause an exothermic chemical reaction. I also talked about the power of suggestion, placebo effects, psychosomatic medicine, and how little we know about the workings of the human brain.

I did not believe it was my role to criticize the efficacy or validity of juju medicine, but instead tried to reiterate the nature of science, and how we as humans can better understand phenomena in the material world by utilizing the scientific method, premised on an empirical approach, involving careful observation, testing, and logical reasoning. I also told the students that whereas science may not have answers to everything, one does not need to rely on a mystical or spiritual crutch for some unexplained phenomenon, merely because a scientific explanation is unavailable at the time. Perhaps some of the students, especially those who had earlier informed me that they were hoping to become brain surgeons or rocket scientists, understood my message, but I fear that for many it was a situation of ears that do not hear.

Because of all the walking to and from school, my generally low carbohydrate diet, and the nematode buddies living in my intestines, I lost about 25% of my body weight during my time in Africa. I arrived in Ibadan weighing 230 lbs, and left two years later weighing 170.

Three weeks before leaving Nigeria, friends and neighbors Ed and Helen went for their mandatory medical clearance. For two years Ed and Helen were meticulously careful in their eating habits. They drank no unboiled or unfiltered water. They refused to eat food purchased from native vendors, instead eating only fruits with a removable skin like bananas and oranges. They assiduously soaked all green leafy vegetables in a Clorox solution for at least thirty minutes prior to consumption. All their efforts were to no avail. At their final medical check the Peace Corps doctor found them ridden with worms, and gave them a quart bottle of a foul concoction labeled "Wormex." The bottle looked like something you'd give to a horse, not a human. They drank the contents with supper one evening, and afterwards, as Ed played his guitar and we sang in their living room, we shared many jokes about Wormex.

When it came time for my medical check before leaving Nigeria four months later, I too had worms, but in spite of my less paranoid approach to eating and drinking, no more than Ed and Helen. Nearly everyone who spends prolonged amounts of time in the tropics, living anywhere other than resort hotels, has to expect to serve as host to some parasite or other. Fortunately I only picked up assorted species of nematodes that are free moving and unattached within the digestive tract, not more serious parasites like filarial worms that cause elephantiasis, guinea worms, Loa Loa worms, heart worms, or a tapeworm that embeds its scolex, equipped with hooks and suckers, into the intestinal lining. Such wormy guests are more difficult to remove from the human body.

Also, in the four months interval following Ed and Helen's medical check, Peace Corps doctors adopted a new protocol for treating intestinal worm parasites. At my medical check, before receiving my final medical clearance, I was prescribed a small container of purple powder. When mixed with water it tasted like a grape soda. Wormex was no longer the worm removing prophylaxis of choice. My grape tasting de-worming cocktail went down easily, effectively narcotizing all the ascarids, whipworms, and other assorted nematodes that called my intestines home. At my next bowel movement we parted company.

Basket weavers in Harar, Ethiopia, August 1965.

With Ugandan friend John Semattire and his son Kazibwe, at their home
in Kampala, Uganda, September 1965

Sitting outside my tent at the tent village in Murchison Falls National Park, Uganda, September 1965.

Three black rhinos inside Ngorongoro Crater, Tanzania, September 1965

Farewell party for Ed and Helen at IBHS, December 1965. Ed (front row, second from right), a Peace Corps volunteer in Nigeria VIII, a group that arrived before mine, taught math at IBHS. His wife Helen, sitting next to Ed, taught math at a girl's secondary school in Ibadan. Seated next to me (far left, front) is English teacher Mrs. Odebunmi, and next to her is the principal of IBHS, S. Akintunde Lasiende, BA (Hons.) Lond.

The women in my HSC (higher school certificate) biology class at St. Theresa's College, Ibadan, January 1966. Each student is modeling a different hair style. Several of these women later pursued advanced degrees at European universities.

With two of the students from my Form V biology class at IBHS at the side of Adeyoola Chambers, April 1966. On my left is Aderibigbe Eboda, and on my right is Adiwaju Oyenola.

Farewell Nigeria! My friend Abiodun Amusan and I at our parting on the front porch of Adeyoola Chambers, Ibadan, May 1966. I have lost fifty pounds since my arrival in Nigeria two years earlier.

24

Homeward Bound

My official termination date from the Peace Corps was April 22, 1966, although I didn't leave the country until four days later. On April 21, 1966 I was the honored guest at the Send Off Programme at IBHS, a gala affair with an opening prayer, speeches, toasts, refreshments, riddles and jokes, the giving of presents, and closing remarks by the principal and several of the Nigerian teachers.

Weeks earlier, I hired a local carpenter to build a large wooden crate for shipping all my personal mementos and gifts for friends back to Long Island via sea freight. The chest, holding all the acquisitions and wonderful memories of my two years in Africa, contained my tailor-made Nigerian clothes and tire sandals, dashikis for my father and brother, glass bead jewelry for my mother and female friends and relatives, decorated gourds, eight thorn carvings, the ibeji carvings, the wood carving of Shango the Yoruba thunder god, and a lovely pair of carved heads of a Nupe man and woman made from ebony wood. The carving of the head of the Nupe man held special memories for me, as I had commissioned a wood carver to make it and had watched him at work for several days, camped out in my back yard, slowly transforming a block of ebony wood into a beautiful carved head with the crudest of tools.

I packed woven bowls and place mats, a floor sweeper made from thin bamboo lengths held together by a handle of colorful woven plastic strips, an oil painting on canvas by the Nigerian painter Christo, records of highlife music by the Nigerian musician Olatunji, the face masks I bought in Ikot Ekpenne, a talking drum, a wooden letter opener with a bird carving handle, several pairs of bird statuettes made from polished cow horns, and a large banner for the NNDP political party

The chest also contained all the objects purchased during my trip to Kano: a blue tie-dyed dashiki, metal spear heads, a bone-handled dagger, a large Tuareg sword in a decorated leather sheath, and three hand made leather ottomans with elaborate stitch work, embellished with tassels and pieces of snake skin.

All the items I bought during my trip to East Africa were in the chest: animal wood carvings from Nairobi, wooden salad sets, two beautiful colorful woven baskets from Harar, beaded necklaces, and the spear purchased from the Masai warrior on the bus to Mombasa. Lastly, there was a large zebra skin drum from Kenya, and the colobus monkey skin acquired in Ethiopia, both purchases which I now deeply regret.

In time I also felt guilty about leaving Nigeria with the ibejis and the Shango carving, both antiquities, and they have since been donated to the collection of the African-American Historical and Cultural Museum in Cedar Rapids.

A day after leaving the crate at a shipping office in Ibadan, I was on public transport heading to Lagos International airport, and out of Africa. I had managed to save only a little money from my in-country daily subsistence allowance of $4.91/day, but I did have a check for $577.81 from the Peace Corps, representing one-third of my readjustment allowance. Also, as part of the "disbursement of funds review" process, I received an additional $422.70 to cover my international travel from Lagos to Kennedy International, the nearest airport to my home address of record.

However, I was not ready to return directly home. Wanting to see some more of the world, I consulted a travel agency. Instead of opting for a direct flight from Nigeria to New York via London, and for only twenty dollars more, I was able to arrange a multi-stopover flight on Dutch KLM airlines, allowing me to visit any eight European cities of my choosing on my return trip home to Long Island.

My plane left Lagos, Nigeria on April 26, 1966, traveling to Tunisia in North Africa. Arriving in Tunis at mid-afternoon, I teamed up with three other Nigeria X PCV's, Carol, Winnie, and Don. We hired a taxi to drive us twelve miles to visit the ruins of the ancient city of Carthage. The next day we departed for Rome.

My itinerary called for nearly three months of travel in Europe, visiting the cities of Rome, Milan, Vienna, Munich, Paris, Amsterdam, London, and Glasgow, spending from one to two weeks in each city. Intending to consult with local tourist bureaus when I arrived at each destination, I planned to stay with local families whenever possible, to see major cultural attractions, visit zoos, and attend performances at opera houses or theatres.

In Rome, I traveled with Carol, Winnie, and Don. We walked the Via Veneto, threw coins into the Trevi fountain at midnight, explored the Coliseum, Forum, and Capitoline and Palatine hills, toured the Vatican, and gawked at the ceiling of the Sistine Chapel. One night, soon after arriving, we went to the Piper Club, a cavernous subterranean discotheque, featuring a rock group called the

Renegades. Thus began my almost surreal transition back to the "modern" world. The scene of hundreds of pulsating bodies, dancing to painfully amplified music on transparent flooring with psychedelic lighting coming from below, seemed curiously more primitive than the world of mud huts and juju medicine I had just left. My travel companions didn't share my passion for classical music, so on three occasions I went to the opera alone, the most memorable being a stirring performance of *Aida* with Leontyne Price. Ten days later I said goodbye to my Nigeria X friends, and began solo traveling through Europe.

In Milan, I found a room in the apartment house of Mrs. Bertoldi on the Via Medici. The following day, May 7, 1966, was cold with drizzling rain, and for the first time in over two years I saw my breath. I overdosed on opera in Milano, going to La Scala nearly every night, the most memorable performance being another rendition of *Aida*, this one starring Grace Bumbry.

From Milan I flew to Vienna, lodging in a quaint attic room in the three hundred year old home of Baroness Lilganau at #15 Krugerstrasse. Each morning I washed in a metal basin and ate croissants with coffee for breakfast, delivered to my garret by the elderly baroness, who walked up three flights of a spiraling white marble stairway with an ornate metal railing from her first floor kitchen. Vienna highlights included a visit to Schonbrunn gardens and zoo, the Spanish Riding School, touring the apartments of Emperor Franz Josef at Hofburg, seeing William Warfield in a performance of *Porgy and Bess* at the Volksoper, and taking the train to the monastery at Melk, then returning to Vienna by boat on the Danube.

Upon arriving in Munich, I found accommodation in the home of a kind German family, the Leibners, who took me on shopping trips and family outings, and generously invited me to join them for family meals. During my week stay I attended more opera performances, including *Martha* by von Flotow, *Otello* by Verdi, and Beethoven's *Fidelio*. I visited the Munich Zoo (Tierpark), and saw the movie *The Sound of Music* in German. Much more sobering was a dark overcast day touring the nearby WW II concentration camp at Dachau.

While resting on a bench in a city park one afternoon, I met Carol, a fellow American solo traveler from New York, and together that evening we went to the Haufbrauhaus, one of Munich's top tourist attractions. Everyone was having a convivial time, drinking steins of beer at long wooden tables, and singing German drinking songs, as buxomly women in traditional Bavarian dress served bratwurst mit sauerkraut, weiner schnitzel, and hot German potato salad. The festive mood changed dramatically when a busload of Texas tourists arrived.

Within minutes the Texans managed to take over the place, making the Haufbrauhaus their own. The largely German audience politely took their provincialistic assault in stride, but for me the whole atmosphere soured when, at their urging, the German polka band started playing their special requests. Whooping it up, and interspersed with a smattering of "yee-haws" and "wah-hoos", the Texans chauvinistically belted out *The Yellow Rose of ...*, *Deep in the heart of ...*, *The eyes of ...*, and so on. I encountered many ugly Americans during my travels through Europe, but Texans, who seem to think that coming from a big state makes them special and better than anyone else, made up a disproportionate percentage.

When I arrived in Paris, I found a room at the Hotel des deux Continents in the St. Germain de Pres area, then quickly headed to the opera house, where I managed to get tickets to that nights performance of a touring Met production of *Barber of Seville*, starring Robert Merrill and Roberta Peters. I thought these famous American singers did a first class job with the Rossini opera, one of my favorites, but the Paris audience found the singing below their standards, and loudly booed. Much to their credit, Merrill and Peters sang beautifully throughout, and smiled to the discourteous jeering and hissing audience at curtain call; a lesser being, like myself, would have given the impolite smug Frenchies the finger.

During my Paris visit, I frequently experienced anti-American sentiments in the form of curtness, and disapproving glances or facial expressions, whilst attempting to use my two years of rusty high school French, as I dined in restaurants and visited the sights. I strolled the left bank of the Seine, climbed the Eiffel Tower, nursed an outrageously expensive glass of wine at a café on the Champs Elysses, photographed the gargoyles on the roof of Notre Dame, lounged about in the Jardin des Tuileries and the Luxembourg Gardens by day, and wandered around the Place Pigalle at night. I spent an entire day at the Louvre, another at the Musee de l'homme at the Palais de Chaillot, and another at Versailles. In the evenings, I attended three performances at the Opera Comique: *Tartuffe* by Moliere, *Lakme* by Delibes, and *La fille de Madame Angot* by Lecocq. While out walking one afternoon, I encountered a stampeding herd of rambunctious Sorbonne students celebrating the completion of their exams, then got caught up in a small riot on the Boulevard St. Germain des Pres.

I thought Paris a lovely city, truly a City of Light, with superb architecture and beautiful parks, but it was not the beauty of Paris, the lovely atmosphere on the banks of the Seine, or the cultural attractions that I most remember, but rather the rudeness of many Parisians. I have had no desire to ever return. The world is an excitingly big place, filled with people who are much more gracious and welcoming than the Parisians I encountered in 1966.

My two weeks in Paris were more expensive than anticipated, and I arrived in Amsterdam with almost no cash. I found a room in the home of Mrs. Vreeswyh at #37 Vossiusstratt, then initiated a survival strategy to carry me through until I received money wired from home (remember, this was back in the dark ages before the advent of ATMs). Every morning, following the meager continental breakfast provided at Mrs. V's bed and breakfast, I walked to the Heineken brewery to take one of the brewery tours. The tours ended in a spacious room, with wooden benches and tables. On the tables were free samples of Heineken beer, and platters of complimentary Dutch cheese and crusty bread. I took a morning tour, an afternoon tour, and one of the last offered evening tours, making certain to try and get a different tour guide each time. In this way, I survived a week in Amsterdam with almost no money.

After each afternoon tour, fortified with beer and food, compliments of the Heineken Brewery Company, I toddled and weaved down the street to the nearby Rijksmuseum, and looked at the wonderful original Rembrandts and other paintings in the museum's collection. I had never seen paintings so large as Rembrandt's famous *The Night Watch* and *The Members of the Cloth Guild.* Much of my time in Amsterdam, thanks to the Heineken brewery, is a bit of a blur, but I do remember being impressed with Rembrandt's paintings, the beauty of the city and its unique system of canals crossed by bridges and carrying boats laden with fresh tulips from the countryside, visiting the Anne Frank house, seeing the Van Gogh paintings at the Stedelijk Museum, and going to the Blijdorp Zoo in Rotterdam.

Then I was off to London. Within minutes after arriving in the city from Gatwick airport, I saw two women in traditional Nigerian dress walking down a street near Trafalgar Square. They were surprised when I greeted them in Yoruba, and responded back. It turned out that they were from Ibadan, and that one had taught for a year at IBHS. I found a small hotel at 143 Sussex Gardens in Paddington, owned by Mr. Murray, and paid for a two week stay. I did the typical touristy things in London, including Westminster Abbey, the Tower of London and the British Museum, but what was especially memorable about my first visit to London (a city I have re-visited many times since), was discovering the criminal court at Old Bailey. I sat in the public visitor's gallery, only planning to spend a short while observing the workings of the British judicial system, complete with wig-wearing barristers, and got completely caught up in the experience.

When I first arrived, the judge was summing up a case involving robbery with weapon, and I decided to listen in on the beginning of the next case heard before the court, one involving robbery with violence. The case was so fascinating that I returned to the Old Bailey and observed the trial from the visitors gallery each day for the next week. The defendant was a young laborer accused of going into a betting shop, demanding money from the woman working there (the plaintiff), then throwing a solution of lye in her face when she started to yell, as he was about to turn and run from the shop. The woman had seen the defendant for only a relatively short time, but gave powerfully convincing testimony about how certain she was of her identification of the defendant as her assailant. She provided the court with a complete and accurate description of the clothes he was wearing, and an uncannily detailed description of his face, including the color of his eyes. At one point in the trial, as the prosecuting lawyer was questioning the young man about the plaintiff's accurate description, and her certainty that he was indeed her assailant, he raised the point of eye color.

"What is the color of your eyes," he asked the defendant.

"I'm not exactly sure," the young man replied.

The lawyer then proceeded to place great emphasis on the vagueness of the man's response, intimating that he was obviously a liar, and by extension guilty.

"What?" the lawyer said in an incredulous tone. "You have been looking at yourself every morning in the mirror for over twenty-four years, and are telling this court that you are not certain of the color of your eyes?"

"Yes," said the young man.

What I found so fascinating about the sudden shift of emphasis to the issue of eye color, which the plaintiff's lawyer considered so incriminating, was that I immediately identified with the accused. I was approximately the same age as he, and if someone had asked me my eye color at that moment I would have answered honestly the same way he had.

Unless they are strikingly blue, I never take note of other peoples eye color, just as I never take notice of sports statistics or the kinds of cars people drive. I had never studied or been aware of my own eyes, perhaps because they are a nondescript pale green. Although I found the case fascinating, I was unable to stay for its conclusion because of time constraints, but I empathized with the accused and hope that justice prevailed.

Other high points of my two weeks in London included a day trip through the lovely Kent countryside, seeing performances of *Arsenic and Old Lace* with Dame Sybil Thorndike and *Day in the Trees* with Peggy Ashcroft, and a performance of *Midsummer's Night Dream* in the open air theatre at Regents Park.

After two weeks in London, I traveled by coach to Swansea, Wales. From there I took a late night train to Fishguard, where I boarded a ferry to Cork, Ireland. Sister Majella had given me the names and addresses of friends and family members in Ireland, so I had many people prepared to welcome me with the wonderful hospitality for which the Irish are known. As I traveled throughout Ireland for the next ten days, I was greeted warmly by strangers wherever I went, one reason I have returned to Ireland many times since.

In Cork, I stayed with some of Sr. Majella's relatives, and had dinner invitations from others. At the convent I met Sr. Fiacre, who drove me to Mt. Melleray Abbey in nearby county Waterford, where I stayed on retreat in the abbey's guest house for several days. Mt. Melleray Abbey is a trappist (Cistercian) monastery, located in a beautiful pastoral setting among the foothills of the heather-covered Knockmealdown Mountains. I welcomed the serenity and contemplative atmosphere of the monastery, and have returned to Mt. Melleray for other visits, in addition to Cistercian monasteries elsewhere, including Caldey Abbey in Wales, and the New Melleray Abbey in Dubuque, Iowa, founded by monks from the Irish monastery in the late 1800's.

Leaving the monastery, I continued exploring Ireland, by train or hitch-hiking, traveling to Killarney, Tralee, Ballybunnion, Limerick, and finally Dublin. Wherever I traveled, I was struck by the natural beauty and the greenness of the Irish countryside, a verdant country aptly dubbed the Emerald Isle.

After several days in Dublin, I took a ferry to Liverpool. From there I took a coach back to London, where I stayed for another week, going to theatres and museums, or pub-crawling with friends and acquaintances from Nigeria. From London I flew to Glasgow, Scotland. I checked into the YMCA, and remained in Glasgow for five days before getting on a plane for the trip home.

25

Re-entry

Whatever reverse culture shock I experienced in Italy or France after two years in tropical West Africa, nothing in Europe fully prepared me for the re-entry trauma I experienced once my plane landed at Kennedy International airport. As I was disgorged into the central terminal building, I imagined myself in an underground chamber of agitated ants, all in panic mode, racing about as if in response to some fear pheromone permeating the air, generated by some unknown intruder. From what emergency were all these people rushing? To what destination were all these hyperactive people so hurriedly headed? In my jet-lagged condition, amidst the frenetic and furious pace in the terminal, I imagined a room full of large molecules, randomly hurtling by one another in Brownian movement fashion, scattering in dozens of different directions because of some energy imposed on them from the outside.

After a two year separation from superhighways, I soon found myself transported in the backseat of an airport shuttle service limo hurtling at breakneck speed on the multi-laned Van Wyck and Long Island Expressways. The world outside the limo windows was a blur. Hands clutching the back seat, watching vehicles impulsively and recklessly lane-changing in order to gain several extra yards of distance, I felt my life had suddenly jolted forward several warp speeds. Why did everything, people, vehicles, scenery, seem to be moving so fast? Why the rush, the atmosphere of urgency? Why are humans willing to acclimate themselves to all sorts of perverse situations, and then call it "making a living?"

Awaiting me in a pile of mail when I arrived home was a certificate of appreciation from the U.S. Government awarded to me

"in grateful recognition of service to our Nation and to the People of Nigeria as a Peace Corps Volunteer"

The certificate was signed by President Lyndon Johnson, and Director of the Peace Corps Sargent Shriver.

Soon after my return, my parents hosted a patio barbeque, attended by my brother, relatives, and neighbors. I kept hoping that someone might ask me a less-than-superficial question about my two years of working and traveling in Africa, but no one did. One of the goals of Peace Corps is for returned volunteers to help their fellow Americans better understand the conditions and circumstances of people of other cultures in other parts of the world. But no one seemed all that interested in hearing about what life was like for Africans. It seemed enough that I had returned home safely, and in one piece; that I had not been eaten by wild animals, or killed by the natives.

And so I re-entered the American mainstream, and have sensed myself drifting ever since. Five months after returning, in January 1967, I received mail from IBHS, forwarded to me by my parents, at my apartment in East Lansing, Michigan, where I was beginning a PhD program at Michigan State. Mr. Adebunmi, the school secretary, sent me the results of the WASC and GCE exams for the 5th form boys at IBHS, the students in my 5th form biology and chemistry classes, that I had taught for two years. Had I taught them well? Had I helped prepare them for their exams, I wondered, as I opened up the envelope and read the exam results for biology, chemistry, Latin, and nine other subjects, printed on the two pages of blue paper inside.

Thirty-nine boys had sat for the exam in December 1966, and of these, thirty-five had passed, a 90% successful pass rate. The highest result in the history of the school. The results for biology were better than for any of the other twelve subjects offered; all thirty-nine boys had elected to take the biology exam, and all had passed, a 100% pass rate, and another school record! It was gratifying to think that I might have played some part in the success of the students on their exams.

Did I have any lasting impact on my students? This is always a difficult question to answer for an educator, because teaching is not like gardening. In gardening, a favorite pastime, and my less expensive alternative to seeing a shrink, you plant a seed and soon thereafter see the rewards of your labor—a lovely blossom, a fruit, a seedling.

But in teaching the feedback is usually slow in coming. Occasionally I hear from a student from one of my classes at the small private liberal arts college in Iowa where I taught biology for thirty-five years. They tell me of a piece of advice I gave them, or a snippet from one of my lectures, that had some lasting effect. In most instances, I am totally unaware that I cast such a little pearl that impacted someone else's life. Did I say that? I really don't remember.

It is always nice for an educator to hear a "thank you," or some words of praise from a former student. It makes the enterprise of teaching, so undervalued in our society, seem worth the while. Sadly, I have long lost touch with all the Nigerian students I taught, and have no way of knowing if my presence at IBHS for two years, my teaching, had any lasting impact on the course of their lives.

When I look at Nigeria today, a nation with so much promise in the 60's, I see a country in flight, without any meaningful or plotted course. Everything seems either to be in disarray, in limbo, or moving backwards. The educational system is in turmoil. Sister Majella left St. Theresa's in 1971, a year before the Federal Government assumed en masse control of all schools in the country. Today, sadly, both St. Theresa's College and IBHS are but shadows of their former selves. Corruption is rampant and regional governors, who should be working to encourage improvements in school buildings, new equipment, newer textbooks, and educational reforms, are siphoning off limited and needed funds for luxury cars and fancy houses. Some schools are so dilapidated, and in such a state of disrepair, that they pose a safety risk to students entering them. The situation is even worse in the northern Muslim states of Kano, Kaduna, and Sokoto, because public education there, especially for women, is even less of a priority.

When sincere and concerned Nigerians, dismayed about the current state of the country's public schools, write about the state of the education system in Nigeria today, they use the same descriptive adjectives: pathetic, disgraceful, miserable, decayed, neglected. When I think of IBHS and St. Theresa's College as I knew them back in the 60's, and the commitment to education that existed in Nigeria then, the future promise of a young democracy in Black Africa, and then read of conditions that exist in the country now, I despair.

And so, what of my Peace Corps experience overall? Simply put, in spite of disappointments and frequent frustrations, the two years I lived and worked in West Africa as a Peace Corps volunteer were two of the most challenging, fulfilling, and memorable of my life, an experience that offered maximal responsibility with minimal supervision. There was no one telling me that I couldn't do something, whether it was teaching swimming, examining urine samples to determine the presence of worm eggs indicating a schistosomiasis infection, or setting up and staffing a school dispensary. If a need existed a Peace Corps volunteer was there to attempt to meet it, provided they had the motivation, the energy, and felt reasonably confident in their abilities to succeed.

In spite of all the hassles and frustrations I encountered living in West Africa, when I remember my African adventures, I do so fondly and thankfully. Learning and understanding another culture best occurs alone, away from one's cultural peers, and that was how I attempted to spend my time in Nigeria. But I found that restructuring one's cultural cognitive universe requires time, and direct immersion in another cultural matrix rarely results in immediate acceptance or understanding. There is no cultural "quick fix." True understanding comes slowly, often painfully so. For myself, my African immersion was too superficial, the time not enough.

I went to Nigeria believing that understanding a different culture can best occur by living and operating from within that cultural context. I was much less conscious then of the fact that as members of a single but multiculturally diverse species we have an obligation to strive for objectivity and truth-seeking in describing and interpreting the cultures of other people, who do not always see the world as we do. The great challenge—largely lost to me then because of my youth and naivete—is to strive for a relativistic interpretation and acceptance of the human condition, that enables us to become more than merely tolerant of the cultural differences that define and separate us. It is sobering to realize how much I missed at age twenty-five, that I would have been more sensitive to and appreciative of now, at sixty-seven.

Humans are the products of instructions encoded in DNA, culture, and circumstance. We all react to challenges, such as leaving one's culture for significant immersion in another, differently. I wasn't able to live my boyhood dream of becoming another Frank Buck. Nor was it a sensible thing to imagine. The world has changed greatly in the last one hundred years, and there aren't that many animals to bring back alive anymore, given our propensity to procreate, to treat Mother Earth as a trash bin, and to view natural landscapes and their resources as a basis for short-term profiteering, with nary a thought given to future generations. Still, I engaged in a different adventure, not as life-threatening as explorer Bucks, but an adventure even so. An adventure of the spirit. To me, the opportunity to set sail on my two year African odyssey was exhilarating. It is the adventure and the excitement of new challenges in an exotically different culture that I remember fondly; the memories involving moments of frustration and disappointment seem much less important now.

Although modern living tends to assign most of us to ruts in terms of work and routine, we should all break free of self-imposed cocoons and make efforts, at all stages of the life cycle, to shake ourselves from our complacency, to accept new challenges, assume new responsibilities, and leave the familiar for new adventures elsewhere. The world cries out for twentieth century explorers of the spirit, and there is much to be done. The Peace Corps still exists for those idealists among us wanting to give back, and it continues to provide a needed service in a world where the disparity between the haves and the have-nots is ever widening. For me, the adventure was in Africa, but adventures of the human spirit need not occur so far from home. They often await no further away than the neighborhood on the other side of town, the house next door.

Now, over forty years, later I continue to struggle with problems of "readjustment" to an America badly afflicted by over-indulgence and over-consumption. We Americans whine too much about the price of gas, not realizing how much the rest of the world pays for the planet's dwindling finite fossil fuels, when we should be liberating ourselves from our gas guzzlers, demanding more energy efficient transportation alternatives, electing leaders with vision, and walking or biking more.

Did I make a difference then? Did I invest my time and energy wisely? Am I making a difference now? These are the questions that sometimes cause fitful sleep or daytime reveries when I contemplate the planet's web of life, insulted as if by delivery of a full round of buckshot, strands broken, poked through with holes.

Long Island used to be beautiful. Then it was covered by roads leading to metastasizing housing developments with a dismal sameness, and vast parking lots servicing architecturally dreary malls and stores filled with stuff to buy. Not too long ago, when my grandparents were raising my mother and father in Bay Shore and Hauppauge respectively, Long Island was a lovely place. Then suburban developers with non-visionary sprawl mentalities ravaged the natural landscape with swaths of concrete for cars, ugly brain-numbing strips of junk-food joints and billboard heavens, shopper's paradises surrounded by vast vistas of parking lots, and sprawling tract housing developments crammed to the gills with characterless houses attached to garages with gaping maws.

Living in the midst of such distressing, depressing, unredeeming manscapes, and burdened with an unhealthy baggage of complacency, gullibility, and apparent inability to recognize word magic when they hear it, most Americans, accepting of mindless growth and manmade monotony, seem oblivious to the growing uglification around them.

The Long Island woodland where I spent so many hours of my boyhood is now a housing development. Few mature trees remain. The adjacent meadow where I tasted wild strawberries and encountered box turtles is totally gone, occupied by an enormous storage warehouse for a furniture store. This is a good thing? In the headlong rush to grow and develop, much of the natural beauty that was Long Island has been lost to what we euphemistically, and by some kind of insidious twisted illogic, call "progress" and "development". Few box turtles now live on Long Island. How could they, with so much of its natural habitats bulldozed away and paved over; with so many roads to safely cross, and so many tire wheels to crush?

So much of twenty-first century society seems fixated on growth and preoccupied with things. As a species we have mind-boggling explosive growth in our own numbers at the expense of planetary biodiversity. Many of the most vulnerable of ourselves are either orphaned, displaced, sick, or starving, at the same time that a vocal minority frets about the destiny of human eggs and sperm, or the fact that the city down the road is growing faster than their own.

The snowline on Mt. Kilimanjaro continues to recede further up the mountain. In only a decade or two Glacier National Park, once with one hundred and fifty glaciers, will have none remaining. The consequences of human-induced global warming that the world is beginning to experience will be not merely inconvenient for us, but catastrophic for our grandchildren.

Why are the holier-than-thou folks, so concerned about the decisions that their neighbors make when it comes to personal and private issues such as sexual behavior, family planning and family size, not more concerned about global environmental issues affecting the future health of the planet, and the lives of their own grandchildren?

In this day and age of overproduction of material goods at our workplaces, over consumption of things in our dwellings, mounting heaps of trash, eradication of tropical rain forests, the killing of our closest living primate relatives for bushmeat consumption, slaughter of innocent persons going to school or to work by fanatics wearing bombs who blow themselves up yelling "God is Great," strip mining of the oceans for their remaining fish stocks, clownish political leaders, and ever increasing assaults upon the life support systems of Mother Earth, I continually find myself asking questions. Why are so many people so self-righteous? Why do we think we have any greater right to exist than any of the other life forms we are eradicating? Why do so many of our leaders assume themselves to be the receptacles of ultimate truth, and proceed to govern with eyes that do not see and ears that do not hear? Why do we behave as if the earth, and all other entities on it, were put here to contribute to our personal needs and selfish pleasures? Just where do we think we are going, so hastily, and with such smug looks of self-assured confidence and determination?

Epilogue

The Years Since

I returned to the States and began work on a PhD at Michigan State University for a year, in September 1966. During my year in Lansing, I met Sharon Sheumaker from Centerville, Iowa, at MSU working on a master's degree in ecology. At the time she must have thought she could put up with me for an extended time period, and rashly accepted my proposal of marriage. We were married in 1968 in West Grove, Iowa.

Relinquishing my fantasy of becoming an opera singer, I completed my doctoral work at the University of Oklahoma, receiving a PhD in Zoology (animal behavior) in 1971. Sharon and I worked as nature counselors for two summers at Camp Chewonki in Wiscasset, Maine. Then we moved permanently to Iowa, where I taught biology for thirty five years at a small private liberal arts college in Cedar Rapids. We had two children, Stephen and Susan, late in life. I formally retired from teaching in May 2005, feeling that three and a half decades of being overworked, undervalued, and underappreciated, was enough. A firm believer in the merits of off-campus study, and the educational value of travel, during my teaching career I often took students off-campus, including marine biology classes on the Belizean barrier reef, hiking and camping on a month-long tour of Texas national parks and wildlife refuges, or traveling around the United States for three weeks visiting twelve zoos as part of a course "US Zoo Odyssey."

For fifteen consecutive years, every January from 1987-2002, I took students to Dog Island, Florida, a barrier island off the northern Florida panhandle, teaching a month-long course "Biology of the Seashore." On Dog Island, I began researching two different symbiotic associations involving marine organisms: hermit crab sponges, and the hermit crabs that often use them as shelters, and a polychaete worm that shares its parchment tube with two different crab species. This research resulted in seven published papers in scientific journals.

Scientists are turned on by the exciting adventure associated with inquiry and investigation of the natural world. Among scientists, field biologists are often a weird bunch, waxing enthusiastic over the most idiosyncratic of Mother Nature's creations, often pursuing greater understanding of nature's mysteries far removed from the affairs of humankind. After fifteen years of working with sponges, and for whatever it's worth, I am an authority on hermit crab sponges, uniquely interesting compact and colorful sponges that provide shelter for certain species of hermit crabs that normally live in snail shells. They are the only sponges that move from one place to another.

An interest in my personal hero, the English biologist Charles Darwin, one of the greatest scientists who ever lived, and a man often maligned by those of little faith who perceive the facts of evolutionary biology as threats to their personal religious beliefs, led me to write a one-man play "Darwin Remembers." I perform the play, upon request, for interested audiences. In 2002, I was named Iowa College Science Teacher of the Year by the Iowa Academy of Sciences. Although no longer "employed" by academia, I continue to pursue personal research interests involving symbiotic associations among certain marine invertebrates, such as small commensal species of shrimp that live inside sponges.

My interest in international travel, engendered by two years of living in Africa, ignited by my travels in Europe in 1966, and motivated by the knowledge that the world is too big a place to be fully experienced in one lifetime, continues to spur me to travel widely and often. I enjoy participating in Earthwatch Expeditions. Many of my travels involve solo long distance hiking, typically off-season, and in off-the-beaten-track locales, finding lodging in monasteries, hostels, or low-budget accommodations. I listen to organ recitals in Baroque churches and attend operas whenever I can.

I own an Amish-built log cabin on 30 acres in scenically beautiful NE Iowa, where I spend much of my time. The area is in Iowa's "driftless zone," a region not covered by the last glacier. The landscape, atypical of most of Iowa, is one of lovely rolling hills, limestone bluff outcroppings, large tracts of forests, and small Amish farms. In my twenty-three acres of woodland, enrolled in Iowa's forest reserve program, I enjoy watching white-tailed deer, wild turkeys, pileated woodpeckers, barred owls, opossums, tree frogs, and other wildlife.

I live off-grid, quite simply, generating what little electricity I use with photovoltaic panels. The cabin has a sturdy outhouse and a roof rainwater collection system. The acreage is managed for increased biodiversity, and as a haven for all things wild and free, including myself; to date over two hundred native trees have been planted and plots of native prairie vegetation will soon be established. Wood ducks and blue-winged teal nest on a small pond surrounded by red cedar, apple, and black cherry trees. In the future, time permitting, there will be a butterfly garden, a rain garden, and a small water hole where amphibians can lay their eggs.

I plant dozens of trees each year, one of the simplest acts of love we can do for the planet and future generations, and hope to plant thousands more before I'm recycled into star stuff. As I often did in my teens, I still occasionally lie on my back outdoors at night contemplating the immensity of the cosmos, asking myself "is this really happening?" I live with Sharon in Cedar Rapids, Iowa.

Map of Africa

The countries I visited, and that are discussed in this book, included:
Nigeria in West Africa; Ethiopia, Kenya, Tanzania, and Uganda in East
Africa; and Tunisia in North Africa

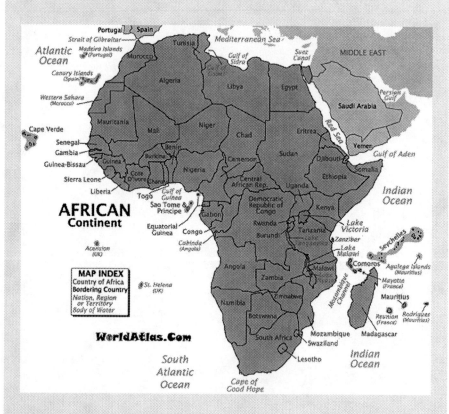

Map provided by: www.worldatlas.com

Map of Nigeria

Many of the Nigerian cities I visited are shown on this map. Some larger cities that I visited, such as Abeokuta, Badagry, Benin, and Ijebu-Ode are not shown.

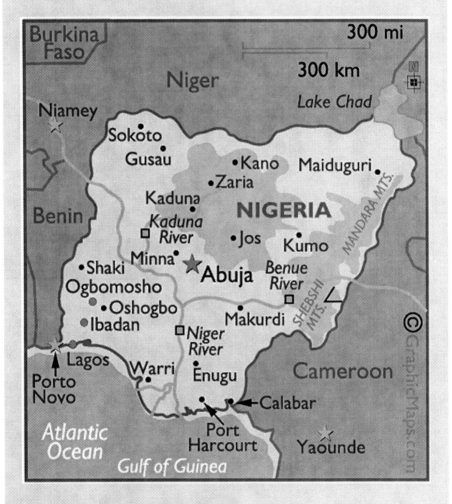

978-0-595-44017-7
0-595-44017-7

LaVergne, TN USA
02 April 2010
177939LV00004B/3/A